Re OCT 10 8
PR apr 30/09
Ql oct 12

Cold Hands, Warm Heart

Cold Hands, Warm Heart

Alaskan Adventures of an Iditarod Champion

By Jeff King

Art by Donna Gates King
Foreword by Joe Runyan

Jack London's quotation on page v represented the writer's personal credo. For more on his extensive writings, visit www.jacklondons.net.

Robert W. Service quotation on page 24 is excerpted from his poem, "The Spell of the Yukon," first published in 1916 by Barse & Co., New York, N.Y.

ISBN 978-0-88240-736-4

LIBRARY OF CONGRESS CONTROL NUMBER: 2007943538

PUBLISHER: Husky Homestead Press
CONTRIBUTING EDITOR: Joe Runyan
EDITOR: Tricia Brown
DESIGNER: Kitty Herrin, Arrow Graphics
MAPMAKERS: Bill Vaughn and Donna Gates King
PRINTED BY: Friesens, Altona, Manitoba, Canada

Husky Homestead
P.O. Box 48
Denali, Alaska 99755
(907) 683-2904; www.huskyhomestead.com

Distributed by Husky Homestead and by Graphic Arts Center Publishing,
P.O. Box 10306, Portland, OR 97296-0306; (503) 226-2402; www.gacpc.com

I would rather be ashes than dust!
I would rather that my spark should burn out
     in a brilliant blaze,
Than it should be stifled by dry-rot.
I would rather be a superb meteor, every atom of me
     in magnificent glow,
Than a sleepy and permanent planet.
The proper function of man is to live, not to exist.
I shall not waste my days in trying to prolong them.
I shall use my time.

—Jack London, 1876–1916

Acknowledgments

A book doesn't just spring into life without the efforts of many people. I want to thank my wife, Donna, not only for these many years of loving support, but also for her wonderful, creative input and the spectacular art in this book.

Thank you to my cousin, Steve Holtze, for that first sled-dog ride.

My appreciation to my hardworking editor, Tricia Brown, and designer, Kitty Herrin, for pulling it all together. Also to "Klondike Kurt" Hellweg, a sincere thanks for your admirable work on my earlier drafts.

To the photographers: Jeff Schultz, my appreciation for many incredible years of artistry covering the Iditarod; Charles Mason, for documenting one of my most fond memories with sled dogs; and Rollie Ostermick, who took spectacular images of freighting in my early years.

To Melissa Hall, thank you for your early work on "Elim."

And finally to Joe Runyan, for years of friendship and good-hearted competition.

Contents

What It Takes to Win

Perhaps you're not inclined to stand on the back of a dogsled and travel 1,100 miles across Alaska wilderness in less than ten days. Few people are. And yet, through the pages of *Cold Hands, Warm Heart,* you'll better understand the experience, from the perspective of Jeff King, the four-time Iditarod champion and arguably the most winning distance musher in modern times.

Jeff has won the Yukon Quest International Sled Dog Race (1989), the demanding 1,100-mile race from Whitehorse, Canada, to Fairbanks, Alaska. He's conquered the 1,150-mile Iditarod Trail Sled Dog Race four times (1993, 1996, 1998, and 2006). And between those long-distance races, he's won innumerable 200- and 300-mile competitions, among them the rugged Kuskokwim 300, which he's won an incredible seven times (1991, 1993, 1997, 2001, 2002, 2003, and 2006).

To sustain this succession of championships with his teams of Alaskan huskies, Jeff has developed a philosophy which at first seems at odds with his extremely competitive personality. An interested fan once asked him, "How do you establish yourself as the leader of your pack of sled dogs?" This is a classic question that presupposes that the musher is the powerful Alpha leader of his huskies and without the musher's total dominance, the team has no momentum and no will to run.

Instead of contradicting the fan's assumption, Jeff explained that the Alaska husky is a wonderful miracle, an animal that was born with an instinct to run and travel. With the proper preparation and training, and by providing all the conditions necessary, Jeff told the group of fans, "I am *allowed* to come along for the ride as a spectator." Then he defined his own role to clear up the "alpha" myth: "I am the coach, the clergy, the manager and clean-up crew."

One of the great rivalries of the Iditarod has been the competition between Jeff King and Doug Swingley from Lincoln, Montana. Swingley won three straight Iditarods following Jeff's victory in 1998 and dominated in 1999, 2000, and 2001. Through those years Swingley always referred to King as his "serious competition."

I once interviewed Swingley and asked him to name a few weaknesses of his archrival. Swingley wisely declined and told me, "I don't want to irritate him. It will only make him work harder." He was, of course, referring to Jeff King's unrelenting focus and competitive drive, reflected not only when he races, but also as he trains and designs strategies and equipment innovations.

To win the Iditarod four times requires strategic insight, training, consistency, and a little self-made luck. The competitive field is deep when one musher, above all others, departs Wasilla on the first Sunday of March, ascends the deep, snow-laden shoulders of the Alaska Range, descends north and west into the extreme cold of the immense Yukon River Basin, crosses a small coastal range to the Bering Sea Coast, battles winds and blowing snow on the treeless tundra of western Alaska, crosses the frozen ocean ice, and trots triumphantly, nine and a half days later, off the beaches of the Seward Peninsula onto the Front Street finish in the old gold boomtown of Nome.

Generally, Jeff likes team speed, but he is characteristically conservative in the first several days of the race and will even stand on the brake, if that is what it takes, to keep his team at a speed he considers within their comfort zone. For the remainder of the race, he will count on having the fastest team on the trail.

Of course, the mushing community is impressed with Jeff's conservative and calculating strategies. One time a pundit asked, "I wonder if someone could be more conservative than King and beat him at his own strategy?" (A question that got a good laugh, but everyone took seriously.) Naturally, Jeff is often asked about his strategy by the media. His typical reply: "There are lots of places to make a move. But the only place it counts to be first is the finish line."

For his own amusement and mental exercise, Jeff enjoys developing a few master innovations. Every year you can bet that there will be a new "showroom" innovation brought out for public viewing at the start of the Iditarod. It could be a new headlight design, a new clothing design for his sponsor, Cabela's, or a radical sled model such as his "caboose" sled, which follows behind his main sled. On one occasion he had his "caboose" outfitted with a straw-filled kennel so that he could he could alternately let his lead dogs rest in comfort while the team was trotting down the trail. Initially, the mushing community looked at his "caboose" sled idea with caution, but today the design is almost universally used.

My favorite King innovation is the "handlebar heater" he unveiled in 2006 (the year of his fourth Iditarod victory). On assignment for a magazine article, I phoned Jeff before the Iditarod start that March and boldly asked if he had any innovations to wheel out before the public.

The phone line was silent. Finally he said, "Well, I've got to keep a few secrets, at least until the start line." What do you say when the master of innovation teases you with a poker player one-liner? Just to keep me sufficiently hooked, however, he offered one more piece of bait: "I will say this—I have a couple of things to help my comfort. I was out testing new prototype gear just yesterday, and I had to laugh out loud. It's almost unfair to be this comfortable."

It wasn't until the second day of the 2006 Iditarod that I saw his new invention. He had reconstructed the handlebar of his sled with copper tubing. Positioned at the middle of his handlebar was a specially designed compact alcohol burner. Of course spectators and the media were fascinated with this magnificent invention and wanted to touch the handlebar with their bare hands in the -10°F temperatures. It was a great diversion for the fans and the media who were watching Jeff feed his dogs in the checkpoint. Occasionally he'd check on his steaming wet gloves that were drying on the sled handlebar. Media updates online read, "King is Smokin' on the Iditarod Trail." Of course the temptation to just "touch it" was irresistible. For the first couple of days Jeff was constantly barking, "Hey, be careful, that handlebar is hot!"

Ultimately I really think King's fascination with invention goes beyond just the things he develops. Rather it is a way of thinking—always looking for a solution to a problem. This may be one of his strongest personality assets. Without consciously realizing it, he is applying the same inquisitive mentality to other aspects of his training.

Most important, he told me, is to grasp that all great mushers understand the mental connection between the musher and the performance of the team. "Even if I have to mask frustration, I always work to stay positive on the outside."

More than anything though, Jeff King likes to have fun with his dogs. He has a great sense of humor. I sat in on an interview in which several reporters were grilling him on some of his ideas and observations. There was a long pause and possibly he was a little exasperated when he replied with a smile, "Well, the dogs still have four legs, and eat out of a dish."

Reading *Cold Hands, Warm Heart*, you will learn about the challenges of racing in Alaska's wilderness and develop an informed understanding of the incredible Alaskan husky. You'll also gain appreciation for the fine art of Donna Gates

Friends and one-time competitors, Jeff King and I were both champions in 1989. King won the Yukon Quest, and I finished first in the Iditarod that year. PHOTO BY POLLY WALTER

King, a widely recognized and highly regarded Alaskan artist who is married to Jeff King. Her detailed drawings and watercolors of sled dogs and Alaska's wilderness are nothing less than spectacular.

Through this wonderful collection of anecdotes, you will also note that I have been given the liberty to make a few of my own comments about Jeff King and his Alaskan huskies.

As you begin this account of Jeff King's life with sled dogs, be prepared to learn a lot about the Alaskan husky, the ultimate long-distance traveler, and the Alaska wilderness. But most of all, just enjoy the ride with Jeff King.

—JOE RUNYAN
1989 Iditarod Champion; Race Commentator and Reporter
Cliff, New Mexico

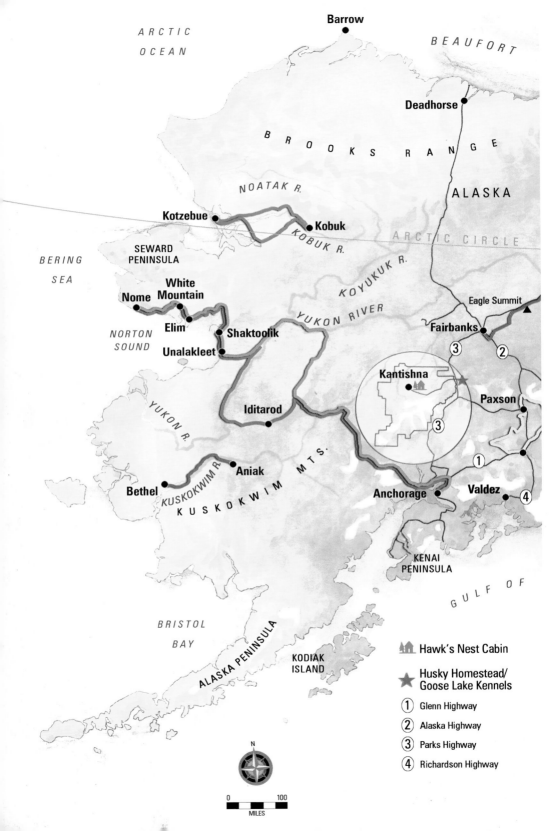

Barrow

ARCTIC OCEAN

BEAUFORT

Deadhorse

BROOKS RANGE

ALASKA

NOATAK R.

ARCTIC CIRCLE

Kotzebue
Kobuk

KOBUK R.

SEWARD PENINSULA

KOYUKUK R.

BERING SEA

White Mountain

YUKON RIVER

Eagle Summit ▲

Nome

Elim

Shaktoolik

Fairbanks

③

②

NORTON SOUND

Unalakleet

Kantishna

Paxson

YUKON R.

Iditarod

③

①

KUSKOKWIM R.

Aniak

KUSKOKWIM MTS.

Bethel

K U S K O K W I M

Anchorage

Valdez

④

KENAI PENINSULA

GULF OF

BRISTOL BAY

ALASKA PENINSULA

KODIAK ISLAND

🏠 Hawk's Nest Cabin

★ Husky Homestead/
Goose Lake Kennels

① Glenn Highway

② Alaska Highway

③ Parks Highway

④ Richardson Highway

N

0   100
MILES

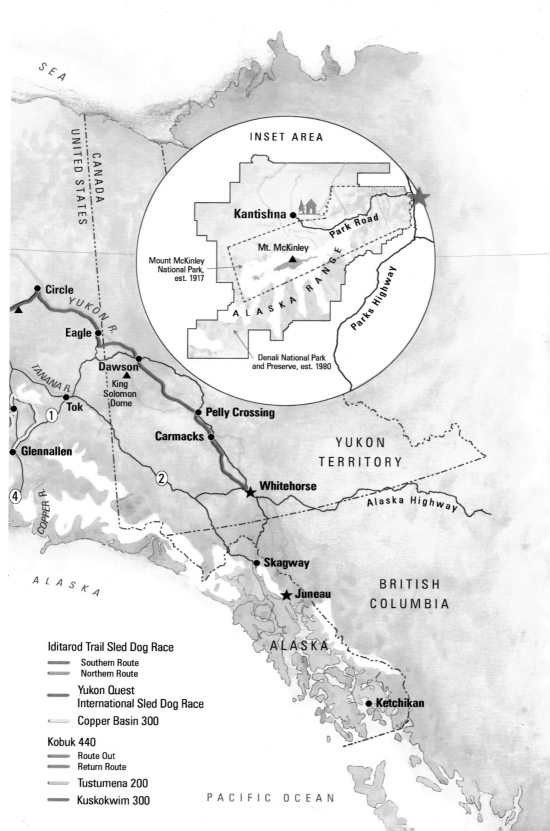

CHAPTER ONE

Breaking Trail

I had just completed my first year of college in the summer of 1975 when I came to Alaska, never dreaming that some-day I'd be racing sled dogs. I had been very involved in sports through the college level, what with playing football and wrestling. Coming out of high school, weighing just 140 pounds, I was recruited to play football.

Can you believe that, a little guy like me playing football in college? Please understand that I would never infer that football players weighing 250-plus pounds aren't competitive, but when you barely tip the scales at 140, there aren't any options—you *have* to be extra-competitive or you're not going to keep all of your body parts, let alone keep your scholarship. Although I at-tended a smaller college, that never deterred me from trying to be the big fish in our little pond, and I went to bed every night thinking about how I could beat the big guys.

However, even given my internal motor and how I thrived operating at high rpm's, when I settled in Alaska, my intentions were not to seek out competition. I wanted to shift a gear or two.

My dream was to live in a log cabin with my dog team, and run a trapline out in the wilderness. It was an idea, a challenge that had been idling in the back of my mind since early childhood and finally revved up into something I just had to do.

Actually, I had been to Alaska once before—when I was six months old. I was born February 6, 1956, in a small logging town in the central California foothills of the Sierras called North Fork. Just six months later, my parents made a bold decision to move to Anchorage with a young family. They were ready for a year of adventure, so my Dad had applied for teaching jobs in both Alaska and Hawaii. Mom later admitted that she was rooting for Hawaii, but a fifth-grade teaching job in Anchorage opened almost immediately—and off they went. (Maybe if Hawaii had won out, I would be surfing and growing pineapples instead of facing into frigid north winds along the coast of Alaska.)

The King family made the long and tiring drive up the Alaska-Canada highway pulling a little house trailer—a true adventure in 1956 when the "Alcan" was nothing more than a long, gravel, two-lane road. My brother Johnny was six at the time and my sister Joannie was just two years old. I was a handful at six months, so the trip was truly a challenge for my parents.

Before we left, my dad's mother, "Granny," presented him with a Winchester .375 H&H Magnum. This rifle had been recommended to her by the salesman at the Sears sporting goods department as the best rifle to have in Alaska. I don't know what she was expecting to happen, but it made her feel secure knowing that her son and his young family had the big gun on board. (Years later my father would give me that rifle when it was clear that I was making Alaska my home. And it sure came in handy in 1981, when a big grizzly showed up in the middle of our dog yard. It is still my favorite moose-hunting rifle.)

My Dad's teaching job was waiting when we arrived in Anchorage, but housing was a problem. The U.S. military had recently deployed 2,000 troops into the Anchorage area. The only place my folks could find and afford to rent was a house with doors and windows that did not shut tight—a terrible construction oversight, especially for an Alaskan home. My mother used to tell the story of squatting down in front of an electrical outlet in their new abode, holding a lit match and watching as the wind, whistling through wall, blew out the flame.

Near panic ensued for the young parents. Once the school year started, the snows started to fly, temperatures dropped, and cold seeped through the cracks as if we were living in a tropical grass hut built on a frozen ice field. My parents, trying to keep three energetic children warm, began having second thoughts about their Alaskan "adventure."

They analyzed their situation and decided to pack up and move home. Mom flew back with my sister and me, while Dad and Johnny raced winter down the Alcan and back to California. Our family settled in the more temperate climate of Marin County, where I spent the rest of my childhood.

As it turned out, my parents bought a house in San Rafael that was just a couple of blocks from the famous Guide Dogs for the Blind—the training facility for seeing-eye dogs. By the time I was old enough to walk to school, I often chose a route that would take me by the Guide Dogs for the Blind. I could see the expansive yard where the trainers worked the dogs, and soon I had a good idea of their daily operation. On weekends and during summer vacations, it was a constant source of interest and a perpetual distraction for a curious little boy.

As a result, I was often late to school and took my time coming home as well. Unafraid about following my interests, I made a lot of friends at the facility. When I saw the trainers and dogs out on the lawn, it seemed reasonable to ask if they needed any help. I suspect on occasion I was a nuisance for some of the trainers, but it made me realize that I had a strong affection for dogs and enjoyed watching them work. At the time, I could not imagine how it would impact me later in life.

As our family matured, Marin County also grew and became more confining, so my parents bought what was then a rural piece of property further north in the hills of Sonoma County. Eight absolutely beautiful acres on the top of a mountain range overlooking Sonoma Valley.

Coincidentally, our property was just a few miles from the magnificent mansion known as the "Wolf House," built by author Jack London. London planned the construction of his home in detail, supposedly built with the highest quality materials and a complete disregard for expense.

Unfortunately, Jack London never lived in the Wolf House. Very near its completion, the house ignited—probably from a pile of rags soaked in linseed oil—and burned to the bare ground on a hot August day in 1913. As I wandered those hills, with some of the land preserved as a park, I often explored the ruins—double-thick concrete walls and decaying reflecting ponds—of Jack London's dream house. Later I became familiar with a famous London quote that described his home in Sonoma:

> The grapes on a score of rolling hills are red with autumn flame. Across Sonoma Mountain wisps of sea fog are stealing. The afternoon sun smolders in the drowsy sky. I have everything to make me glad I am alive. I am filled with dreams and mysteries. I am all sun and air and sparkle. I am vitalized, organic.

Our home in the Sonoma hills was a dream come true for a ten-year old boy who loved to roam with his dog. I often visited the Wolf House ruins and imagined I knew just how London felt. I became a big fan, and I read and often memorized his accounts of Alaska, the Yukon, and the Klondike.

In addition, I was a huge admirer of Davy Crockett and Daniel

Boone, and had my own cap with a fake raccoon tail hanging off the back. As a kid I was known for bringing home pockets bulging with mementos of my hikes, including wild creatures—usually alive. Mom became very cautious when checking pockets and preparing my clothes for the wash. Tromping through the hills with our family pet, Sam, and quietly influenced by Jack London's tales of the Arctic, I thought of adventures of my own.

I became fascinated with my place on the planet and how I might exist self-sufficiently. These were dreams that started in my childhood. My favorite book had been *My Side of the Mountain* by Jean Craighead George, and it described how a little boy named Sam Gribley lived in a hollow tree with his pet falcon, which would help him catch rabbits. He learned to live comfortably from the land, picking acorns, catching deer, and making his own tools. He loved his family and would sneak back to his home once in a while, to check on them from afar. It was a wonderful story that enriched my dreams of living off the country.

I also had a cousin in Minnesota who ran a trapline and caught skunks and raccoons. As a ten-year-old boy I was totally fascinated by my older cousin's efforts to harvest fur and make his own clothes, coin purses, and gear pouches. So I constructed my own trapline in the Sonoma hills on the weekends when the family visited our new property.

Knowing I had to go back to school on Monday, I worked hard to set up my trapline and dismantle it every weekend. I would start to work on a Friday night, putting out my trapline, and get up early on Saturday and Sunday mornings to walk and check my traps. From a ten-year-old's perspective, this went on for what seemed my entire life—and I never caught a thing. However, it did not seem to matter—the anticipation was incredible. I read every book I could on trapping lore and followed detailed instructions to make concoctions of smelly baits for my traps, which made my Mom shudder. Sam, wagging his tail, accompanied me on every walk through hillsides covered with manzanita, bay, oak, and towering fir trees to check the line. He seemed to share and understand my passion. The Sonoma hills were rich with wildlife and natural surprises.

I often wish I could give that childhood of adventure to others. Reflecting on my boyhood wandering those oak woods, it was a wonderful feeling of freedom and accomplishment.

I was too young to carry a gun, and it never occurred to me what I might do if we actually caught some game. On one of those many weekend ventures, I went down to check a live-trap that I had baited with one of my concoctions. The trap was designed to close a wire door to catch game alive, and sure enough, that morning I found a young gray fox looking up at me from inside the trap. I was elated, ran home to wake my Mom and Dad, and give them the great news that I had actually caught something.

My Dad went with me to the trap, shared in all the excitement, and helped me retrieve the wire-frame with the fox in it. However, we were now faced with a monumental problem that I had not considered in great detail. What are we going to do with it? I hadn't thought about that.

As an adult who has achieved some success as an entrepreneur, I can look back and laugh at my beginnings in the business world. We took that fox back to our big house in Marin County, and with the help of my brother and sister, set up a viewing area in our atrium, complete with signs and a security guard. For the next week, I charged neighborhood kids up and down the street a nickel to come see my fox. It was a big attraction, and I had lines of kids waiting to take a look. My sister importantly separated each coin from its owner and directed the anxious voyeurs to step behind the curtain, a stained sheet suspended by some clothesline. I stood, my fake coonskin hat atop my head, posed beside the fox in the live-trap, and with puffed-up pride, described to our "guests" my heroic antics on the trapline. I was in my element.

Some aspects of the trapper's responsibilities still eluded me, and I wasn't prepared to dispatch the animal. The fox soon went to live in a wildlife park in San Rafael.

Over the next couple of years, during weekends on the mountain at our Sonoma property, I did catch another fox and later a bobcat. I still was not old enough to go through the hunter-safety course so I could carry a gun. Therefore I had a dilemma when I found my next trapped fox. After some deliberation, I ultimately gave the fox a whack on the head with a stick, put him in my pack and continued checking my line. After about a mile, however, I felt a disturbance in my pack and looked behind to see a dazed fox poking out his head and peering at me over my shoulder. I quickly slipped off my pack, ran to a nearby stream and dove in. I submerged the fox, pack and all, underwater.

After high school, I spent a year at Shasta College, a small junior college in northern California, and had a successful sports career wrestling and playing football.

Sports fans will notice that you never say, "I play wrestling." Wrestling is serious, one on one. You don't "play" wrestle—you just wrestle. But I was small, and playing football with some guys more than twice my weight often was like wrestling for me. It was my strategy to be very serious and competitive to get through a football practice in one piece. I loved it, but I had to stay sharp and focused in both sports during that year at college. At age nineteen, however, I had an irresistible opportunity to go to Alaska and work for the summer. I left the world of school and competitive sports, at least for a while.

Three other college kids also jumped on the bandwagon to get summer jobs at Mount McKinley National Park, now known as Denali National Park and Preserve. Together we drove up to Alaska in a Chevy pick-up, trading off driving and riding in the back of the truck. It was a long trip, and we almost never

The Denali Web, 1994 watercolor.

Denali National Park Commemorative print. The image depicts the predator-prey relationship that is in natural balance within the Park. This delicate balance supports the web of life for all of these Interior Alaska species.

stopped—with two in the cab and the other two sleeping in the truck bed. It was a driving marathon that I have not been tempted to duplicate. We arrived at the Park on June 9, 1975.

I remember arriving at Denali in daylight bright enough to read a book—at twelve o'clock midnight—and being amazed seeing the sun just hovering on the horizon—not sure whether it was setting or rising.

I was immediately stuck on Alaska.

JOE'S NOTES

Take note, this is a little story of destiny. In the crucible of sports, an athlete finds that success is not necessarily related to overwhelming size and strength on the football field.

Wiry, tough, very competitive—like Jeff King—might make a musher.

CHAPTER TWO

Doggone Destiny

During my first winter in Alaska, I lived in a tiny cabin at Carlo Creek, just fourteen miles south of the Park entrance. It so happened that across the highway there lived a dog musher. Dennis Kogl had earned some local fame for his expertise with his freight team by hauling thousands of pounds of provisions each spring to the base camp of Mount McKinley for mountain climbers. I was enthralled and inspired.

The following winter I acquired my first sled dog—by way of California. My brother Johnny had brought Angie all the way up from San Francisco, where he had picked her out at the local animal shelter. I have to admit that she wasn't exactly "a catch," but I didn't know that at the time. I built my first sled out of an old pair of downhill skis, harnessed Angie to the front, and my adventures in dog mushing began.

I spent one of my winters living in a wall tent with my fledgling dog team that had been cobbled together, including a stray from the neighboring village of Cantwell and several young pups from local mushers in the Denali area. I can only imagine if one of my kids would have written home and said, "I am going to live three months alone in a wall tent in the middle of Alaska with my dog team." My parents supported me, however—but they must have been mortified.

I had an AM radio set-up for a daily check on the world at my tent camp close to the northern boundary of Mount McKinley National Park near the old mining community of Kantishna. Otherwise it was very quiet as I spent my days driving dogs on a trapline across tundra and through black spruce forests. I was in an extremely remote area, with few winter inhabitants. I was alone, but I wasn't lonely, as I tested the reality of the experience against my childhood dreams.

Three months in the wilderness was a life-changing experience for me. I had a chance to do a lot of thinking and read some great books at night—with a Blazo Coleman lamp burning for light— while I tried to keep warm in my sleeping bag at forty below zero. One book in particular, *Mawson's Will: The Greatest Polar Story Every Written*, by Leonard Bickel, was an incredible account of survival in the Antarctic that, by comparison, was making my experience seem like a stay at The Ritz. This book inspired me to contemplate my own experience and put it in perspective. With good skills and planning, even the coldest weather and adversity could be overcome—an attitude that has stuck with me to this day.

My novice dog team was beginning to develop with my full attention every day. By the time I emerged from the woods three months later, I was starting to form a group of well-trained dogs that could travel with speed and power. After three months of what I initially considered just an enactment of a childhood dream to live a subsistence lifestyle, I had a healthy dog team, a small sack full of marten pelts, and had survived the Alaskan cold of winter with simple, basic equipment. Although it was not a life I would choose to live forever, those three solitary months forced me to consider a direction in my life. It also was an advanced education in the behavior and capabilities of the remarkable Alaskan husky.

On my return trip back to my cabin, I ran smack-dab into a dog race. A sign at the local post office advertised "Dogsled Race." It was scheduled for the coming weekend. I started to think, *My team is in good shape and has had lots of training over the last three months—I should enter the race.* Plus my competitive athletic instincts were being re-energized, and I figured I better not pass this up.

I entered that race. Wide-eyed and hanging on for dear life, I could tell that my dogs loved going fast with the excitement of other dogs around them, and I clearly enjoyed competing with the other teams and the mushers. I knew I was hooked on racing sled dogs. My size and athleticism, contrary to playing football, gave me an advantage over many of these mushing competitors. I had a combination of the skills needed for competitive dogsled racing: I thrived on competitive sports, I had strong outdoor skills, and I had a deep love for animals and dogs in particular. It seemed I had been prepared through the experiences of my childhood to be lured down this trail.

On a grander scale, I started dreaming about running the Iditarod, the race I heard about on my AM radio while on the trapline. Some really crazy mushers, I had heard, were racing over a thousand miles on old gold-mining and trading trails from Anchorage across western Alaska to Nome. I tried to find as much information as I could about the novel, long-distance race that began in 1973, and started thinking seriously of running the Iditarod.

As it turned out, 1980 was a big year for me and these life-changing events would secure my future in Alaska. I acquired my own five-acre piece of property that would be the present location of my kennel and home, and also entered my first Iditarod. I knew that I wanted to build a bigger home overlooking the lake on the property

I purchased, but I did not have the money to do it right then, and I did not want to do it alone.

Instead I built a simple, 12-by-16-foot, one-room cabin on the edge of the property. It still stands there today, a monument to my early years in Alaska. This was also my operations center for training to run in my first Iditarod.

Often the dogs and I would train on the Park road traveling from the main entrance to the interior of the Park. If you have ever taken a tour through Denali Park during the summer, you would have been on the same road that I have used as a winter training trail—although in winter, the road is buried in snow and closed for vehicular traffic.

Of course the National Park Service has had its own kennel and dog teams for years. Initially the teams were used for patrolling, but by 1980 they had become a sort of living memorial to the early history of the park. Today the sled-dog kennel is operated as a living history demonstration for summer visitors and tourists to the Park and is maintained during the winter. Hired personnel take care of the kennel and do some training, but the operation relies on organized volunteer help to train the dogs. The volunteer position was a coveted job during those times in the early '80s, and many people applied to come to Alaska in the winter to drive the Park Service's dog teams. Through the grapevine of our small community, I heard there was a new gal over at the Park Service who was volunteering at the kennel.

At that time, mail arrived by the Alaska Railroad two times a week, and there was no phone service for most of us. Our little post office, in the old depot building by the rail siding, was open on those days for two hours in the afternoon. Consequently, picking up mail became a social affair. By the end of the winter, you were likely to get to know just about everyone in the community at the post office. It was a good time to catch up

Iditarod Dream, 1983 watercolor.

Dilly and Speedy competed in the first Jeff King Iditarod team in 1981. This water-color image was created in Minnesota to raise funds to race again. This was Donna's first limited-edition fine art print.

with old friends—"Hey, what have you been up to since the last time the mail came?"—and you soon knew just about everyone in Denali by sight. On one of these mail deliveries, I noticed the young woman who had volunteered for the Park Service kennel position, but we had not been introduced. I made a mental note to be sure that an introduction would happen soon.

Preparing for the Iditarod was my full-time focus during the winter of 1980–81. I used the Park road regularly for training because I could get in some long, uninterrupted training runs—similar to what I expected to find on the Iditarod Trail. One training day, I was going out on the trail and saw fresh tracks from a sled dog team ahead of me. It was not difficult to read the tracks, especially if you use a trail regularly, and intuitively I could tell that this team, probably from the Park Service, was not far ahead.

Quite honestly, the Park Service teams were notorious for being unmanageable and just barely trained. In all fairness to their hired kennel trainers, part of the problem was that the dogs never had the same driver and, even more, their volunteers had less experience than the dogs. With the constant rotation of volunteers, it wasn't hard to appreciate the dogs' reaction—they quickly analyzed the situation and knew exactly what they could get away with. In many cases, the dogs did what they wanted to—which, in human terms, could be disastrous.

As I examined the tracks, I wondered what an encounter with a Park Service team might be like that day. I was getting my team in order for the upcoming race, and I couldn't afford a tangle or to have a snappy Park dog nail one of my Iditarod dogs and put them out of training with an injury. In the sled-dog racing game, it's expected that the teams are trained to pass on their best behavior and especially do not bite. In fact, an "alligator" dog in a team is reason enough for a Race Marshal to issue a strong warning or even disqualify a musher from the race. Any musher who has a reputation for driving a poorly trained team doesn't receive a lot of sympathy from anyone.

But this was different. This was the Park Service and I had to be alert for my dogs. A small silhouette appeared in the distance, and I could see that I was following the team and musher traveling on the trail ahead of me. That was good, and I was relieved because it meant that we were not going to pass head-on.

My team was trotting smoothly and quickly gaining on the distant team. By the time I caught up, the Park team was just beginning to take a fork in the trail I had not planned on using. As they veered off to the side trail, I thought if the timing was right, I could pass without getting close to the other team at all. They disappeared from sight as I advanced and then reappeared. My attitude changed as I realized that the Park team had made a loop and was now barreling straight back down the trail toward my prized Iditarod huskies.

It was obvious that this outfit was completely out of control, and the volunteer on the sled runners, who appeared to be a slightly built woman, was probably out of her league. Her team of Park Service juvenile delinquents was not only charging downhill toward us, but also had gravity on their side. Heading back to the Park Service barn, they ran like a team of wild horses.

One of the few problems with training on the snow-covered Park Service road was stopping the dogs. Most mushers have a "snow hook," a two-pronged anchor of sorts attached by a rope to the main towline of the dogs. If snow conditions are hard enough, or if there is a spruce tree or an old stump available, you can set the snow hook and stop the team. However the Park road is twenty feet wide, making the trees out of reach, and the snow is rarely firm enough to hold "the hook" in the deep, soft powder.

Another option is to stand on the sled brake with all your weight to slow the team, but unless they want to stop, there is little you can do to deter almost six hundred pounds of dog power.

New Friends, 1990 pencil.

Pencil drawing of daughter Tessa, joined by some buddies on the steps of Harold Eastwood's workshop.

"Stopping" the team can be a big problem, especially when there's a lot of excitement. I could tell that the small woman behind the Park Service team was not going to stop and was hardly slowing the battle charge heading my way.

I accepted the inevitable. We were heading for a first-class head-on, out-of-control, nose-to-nose collision with the Park Service team. My team was moving with the grace and discipline of a West Point drill squad as the approaching Park team charged at us like second-graders headed to the playground at recess. As my team tried to make a smooth pass, the Park Service team reacted like a local gang spoiling for a fight. In seconds we were tied in a giant and confusing granny knot. It was a mess.

The frantic young lady tried to remain calm and figure out what to say to her dogs and what to say to the musher of the other team. It was certainly obvious to her that the other musher had more experience and knowledge. Was he going to be mad, nice, helpful, or completely disgusted? The fact was, this was my first formal introduction to my wife-to-be. Fortunately my behavior was exemplary.

Donna and I eventually got our teams untangled. We saw each other off and on during the rest of the winter while I trained hard for my first Iditarod in March of 1981. Following the completion of the race, she returned for another year as a naturalist with the Park Service. This, plus working as a freelance artist, kept her busy in Alaska until the following year when she was offered a staff position as a medical illustrator at the prestigious Mayo Clinic in Minnesota. That following fall I farmed out my small dog team to a friend and followed her to Minnesota for a few months.

Within days of arriving in Rochester, I tested for and received my license to drive interstate semi trucks, an adventure in life in America that would add a few interesting experiences to my list. I found myself driving "swinging beef" out of Texas and transporting loads of unpalleted boxes of Malto Meal to Denver (which would take me over eight hours to unload by hand, box by box). There I was, sneaking through Illinois on back roads in the dead of night because of exceeding the legal weight limit. Another time, I found myself hopelessly lost in Memphis and trying earnestly to understand driving directions from the locals. I believe my willingness to leave Alaska and bounce around the Lower 48 in a semi truck convinced her, and me, that we were truly meant to be. We were married in a small New England church near Donna's folks' on a spectacular autumn day in October of 1983.

While Donna worked out the final months of her job at Mayo, she completed a watercolor painting depicting the vivid action of my two favorite sled dogs, Speedy and Dilly, straining in harness. It was printed in La Crosse, Wisconsin, and the proceeds were earmarked to fund my next Iditarod Trail Sled Dog Race. It was her first limited-edition fine art print and was titled "Iditarod Dream."

As fate would have it, shortly after we were settled back in Denali and while checking the mail at the McKinley Post Office on train-day, the Fairbanks newspaper boasted a headline that read "New 1,000-Mile Sled Dog Race." The Yukon Quest International Sled Dog Race was born. The creative inspiration for this new event was the result of the mushing fever that was sweeping the state. The race would begin in Fairbanks, Alaska, travel historic gold-rush trails north to Circle City and up the mighty Yukon River through places like Slaven's Cabin, Trout Creek, and the village of Eagle, en route to the famous Klondike gold fields surrounding Dawson City. From there the trail would continue over King Solomon's Dome, Scroggy Creek, through the village of Carmacks and on to the finish line in Whitehorse, Yukon Territory. The trail was steeped in history that had been the inspiration for many Jack London stories that I had read as a boy. This new trail beckoned.

I left the start line of the inaugural Yukon Quest in February

1984, and continued to make this race my focus for the next seven years. The Yukon Quest quickly grew to a premier long-distance event through very challenging terrain with distances between checkpoints that reach well over 200 miles. I eventually won the Yukon Quest in 1989 after a harrowing, near-death dunk in the Yukon River at -38°F.

Those years of living in a small cabin without electricity or running water saw our family grow with the birth of our three beautiful daughters, Cali in October of 1984, then Tessa in June of 1986. Our youngest, Ellen, was born in January of 1992. All three girls have grown up with puppies as friends and huskies as companions.

As for Donna and I, the sled dogs not only introduced us, but they have also been a huge part of our life as we worked together to build a home, raise a family, create a business, and sculpt a future.

Joe's Notes

The first Iditarod, a tribute to the Alaskan husky and an effort to preserve the mushing tradition, was organized in 1973. Dick Wilmarth won the event in twenty days. Many Alaskans initially doubted that sled dogs could travel over a thousand miles. What followed, however, was an unanticipated fascination from mushers all over the world, with the adventure and race known as the Iditarod. Mushers discovered that the indomitable Alaskan husky could travel 1,100 miles—and do it in half the time. Jeff King's fastest winning time was 9 days, 5 hours, 43 minutes.

CHAPTER THREE

Christmas on the Trapline

The tradition of gold-mining and trapping sustained many of the early pioneers in Alaska. Even today the extraction of gold and the harvest of furs is defended by many Alaskans as a legitimate way of making a living in rural parts of the state, more commonly called the "Bush." If done properly and ethically, the wilderness is left more or less intact, and in the case of trapping, the population of the fur-bearing animals soon rebounds, leaving an inconspicuous mark on the environment. Although we may disagree on the political process that establishes procedures for harvesting Alaska's resources, no one can deny that for many Alaskans, mining and trapping are an important part of the culture in the Far North.

This self-determined, rugged individualist kind of lifestyle has had a certain attraction for me since childhood. When I moved to Alaska as a young adult, I had a vision of living in a tent or a log cabin with my sled dogs and running a trapline. Was it my fascination with the self-sufficient mind-set of Alaskans that drew me to the outdoors? It could be, but I knew one thing for sure—I wanted to experience it. I remember being mesmerized by a powerful verse in Robert Service's famous poem "The Spell of the Yukon":

> *There's gold, and it's haunting and haunting;*
> *It's luring me on as of old;*
> *Yet it isn't the gold that I'm wanting*
> *So much as just finding the gold.*
> *It's the great, big, broad land way up yonder,*
> *It's the forests where silence has lease;*
> *It's the beauty that thrills me with wonder,*
> *It's the stillness that fills me with peace.*

As I reflected on that poem, it wasn't necessarily trapping for furs that fueled my dream. I just fantasized about living the lifestyle of a trapper and a musher. Because of that reoccurring dream—long before I established my kennel, or built my cabin, or met my wife—I had made plans to spend a winter just outside the north boundary of what was then known as Mount McKinley National Park, in an area drained by the Kantishna River. Locals knew it as the Kantishna and as an area rich in wildlife.

I discovered Kantishna through my neighbor, Harold Eastwood. Harold was old enough to be my father, but over time he had become one of my closest friends. He was a true outdoorsman, having spent many years hunting mountain lions in the Colorado Rockies, and later hunting big game in Alaska. He had hunted moose in Kantishna, up the Clearwater River, and described to me a place that would be bountiful in both furs and solitude. "Just head up Moose Creek, past the Glen Creek mining area, then up over the pass to Myrtle Creek. I know you'll find a great spot to set up your wall tent."

I heard the echo of Robert Service in Harold's words, and it sounded perfect!

Old Friends, 1990 pencil.

The companion piece for New Friends. That's Harold Eastwood outside his workshop with Sammy and Solo, our old leaders.

So early in the fall of 1979, before snow closed the Park's gravel road, I drove the ninety miles from the east entrance of the Park to the famous landmark of Wonder Lake at the westernmost end of the Park road. Mount McKinley towered over that lake like a giant white ghost in the distance, while the tundra was brilliantly splashed with the fall colors of purple, yellow, orange and red—and scattered groves of the green-needled black spruce accentuated the landscape. I imagined this same vista covered in a white, pristine blanket of snow later that fall when I would return—mushing my dog team.

Wally and Jerri Cole, the owners of Camp Denali, had generously offered the use of their little cabin as a cache for my winter supplies. Aptly named "The Hawk's Nest," it was built on a little knoll above Wonder Lake, and its front window gazed directly at the majestic Mount McKinley—the tallest mountain in North America at 20,320 feet. It was here that I cached my carefully selected winter supplies and gear. Although I was working with a very limited budget, I made sure that I stashed enough of what I would need for the three months I planned to be completely self-sufficient. So after securing the Hawk's Nest, I hurried home, where I eagerly organized my sled, gear, and dog team.

And then I waited.

You can imagine that I was not exactly the poster boy of patience as I waited around for it to snow. Not just snow, but snow enough to make the Park trails passable by a dog team, enough that I could finally begin my long-anticipated adventure.

The day finally arrived when I could "pull the hook," releasing my team and me down an unfolding trail of adventure that I had anticipated for most of my life. It took three days for us to get to the far end of the Park, stop to gather additional supplies at my cache at the Hawk's Nest, and then continue another 10 miles to the area where I planned to set up camp. The fall colors were now blanketed in snow, the daylight had grown shorter, and the November temperatures were often well below zero.

After a long day of snowshoeing a trail from the Glen Creek mining claims, I found a spot at the mouth of Myrtle Creek as the willowy maze emptied into the Clearwater River—smack dab in the middle of where Harold suggested that I should camp. I set up my canvas wall tent below the only spruce trees that I could find in the dense willow jungle of the creek bank. Exhausted, I fed the dogs and fell asleep making plans to improve my camp and amenities the next day.

I was snugly tucked into my warm sleeping bag when I awoke in pitch darkness to complete confusion. The ground was undulating up and down under my caribou-skin sleeping pad. The walls of the tent were increasing their staccato slapping sound as a rapidly advancing wind screamed down from the surrounding mountaintops. The roots of the spruce trees, which were supporting my tent, began to strain as the wind buffeted the boughs. The walls billowed like sails on stormy seas. As the tree leaned away from the wind, my sleeping pad levitated as the roots stretched in a valiant effort to keep the swaying trunk firmly connected to the earth.

It wasn't long before the tent's walls ripped free of their temporary guys, and flapped crazily—leaving me exposed to the cold, biting night air. Cocooned in my sleeping bag, I frantically reached out and gathered my clothes, parka, mitts, and anything else that was threatening to blow away on my first night out. I had made a rookie mistake by not taking the time to select a proper campsite and secure the guy ropes to withstand such savage weather. It was my first sobering reminder that I was most certainly alone, and that small mistakes had the potential of becoming big problems very quickly.

Needless to say, I spent the following day hunting for a more protected campsite and finally settled on a spot downstream from the mouth of Myrtle Creek, in a small, unnamed gully just upstream from Moonlight Creek on the Clearwater River.

A wall tent can be quite comfortable—as long as there is a lively fire in the stove. Spruce boughs on the floor make a nice soft carpet, a Coleman lamp is good enough to read by, and an AM radio wired to the ridgepole of the tent, with a long antenna wire, is the trapper's connection to the outside world. Picketed outside on their own bed of spruce boughs was my main social circle for the winter: a team of sled dogs. I learned that when chores are done, and the fire goes out, it's best to be comfortably tucked inside a good, warm sleeping bag. The location I settled on was spectacular, and I felt as rich as any king with my dog team and my tent for the next three months.

A typical workday on the trapline was everything that I had imagined in my childhood fantasy. Technically, my job was to break out a trail and progressively lengthen my trapline. I was primarily looking to trap marten, the rusty red/brown fur-bearing weasel (actually, a distant relative of the mink). The marten is Alaska's most abundant furbearer and is marketed as "American sable." And with the right conditions over the summer, marten populations can explode. They thrive in the black spruce and birch stands of Alaska's Interior. Marten-trapping and dog-mushing work especially well together because you can make sets alongside the dog trail. Unlike other furbearers, such as the cautious wolverine or the extremely perceptive wolf, marten seem to disregard the scent of sled dogs and are curious enough to travel on or near the same trails without any alarm or concern.

Marten are curious, opportunistic feeders. They will eat everything from blueberries to mice and squirrels. Over the years, trappers have successfully harvested marten with bait ranging from rotten salmon or whitefish to raspberry jam. One of the most common ways to set a marten trap is to first chop down a 15-foot spruce tree, typically 2 or 3 inches in diameter. When felling the spruce, you need to leave the stump well above the surface of the snow, usually at about armpit level. The next step is to trim the remaining trunk of its branches—with your trusty Hudson's Bay ax, of course. After you've fashioned a sturdy pole, you drive the narrow end into the snow and support it on the stump, leaving a couple of feet of the thickest end of the tree cantilevered in the air. From a distance, it will look like a pole leaning at about a 45-degree angle. Without going into serious detail, next imagine that you wire a trap to the upper section of this pole and place some bait at the very end of the pole. To get to the bait, the agile marten, which regularly climbs trees to catch squirrels, will have to scurry up the pole and over the trap. That's the theory of a "pole set," a quick and effective set used often in Alaska to catch marten. If a marten is trapped, the trap and marten will fall off the pole and hang by a trap chain, making it easy to see while you are approaching the set with your dog team. In the cold, the marten will quickly expire, and the catch will be secure from mice, at least for a while.

Although there was obviously the daily maintenance of my trapline, my true preoccupation and primary interest clearly revolved around the relationship I began to develop with my sled dogs. The dogs and I traveled together through spruce forest and open tundra, across lakes and streams, and never saw another human that entire winter while working the line. Besides the pure satisfaction of traveling with them, I also began to appreciate the subtleties of observing and just living with them day in and day out. I began to understand their needs, their behaviors, and their personalities. It was an enlightening experience that solidified and deepened my connection with the dogs and heightened my ability to communicate and understand them. It created the basis of my relationship with sled dogs that I clearly continue to enjoy and explore as the years "mush on."

Now the only people within reach by dog team from my camp were a couple who lived the exact life I was trying to sample— they mined gold in Kantishna in the summer and trapped in the

Fresh Tracks, 1990 watercolor.

With Mount McKinley and the McKinley Bar in the background, the team takes a break from breaking trail as the musher inspects the moose tracks. Harold Eastwood, wearing the moosehide mitts given to Jeff at the 1989 Yukon Quest start, served as the model. The white moose in the spruce trees represents the moose that Harold shot in the Kantishna in the 1970s.

winter. These friends, Dan and Berta, had chosen an adventurous, but secluded life, and were content to spend most of their year at their remote cabin.

Conveniently, their place was about 10 miles from my tent camp and less than a mile from my cache of supplies at the Hawk's Nest. In time, it became my routine to head downriver, resupply, and then spend the night in the Hawk's Nest cabin every week or so.

Besides the necessary restocking, I began to look forward to this trip because it was my only contact with people. Mostly I was alone, usually out in the woods checking traps with my dogs, or snugly tucked in my tent. It was such a pleasure to report to Dan and Berta what I had seen on the line or caught in my traps. For me, our visits became a welcome interaction with good friends.

On the flip side, despite the seclusion they chose, I'm pretty sure that Dan and Berta likewise began to look forward to those days when they knew I would be coming back down the trail to Wonder Lake and my supply cache. The signal of my arrival was smoke billowing from the smokestack of the Hawk's Nest cabin. Dan, in particular, watched for it with a keen interest that went beyond our growing friendship. Dan also knew that the little knoll upon which my cache sat was the only place around for miles where his brand-new radio could receive a signal. Dan's receiver had this interesting capability of not only capturing AM and FM radio signals, but it could pull in the audio tracks from a television signal as well.

Dan loved to visit the Hawk's Nest on my resupply days—and he would always be sure to bring his fancy new radio along. Together we would search the airwaves to "see" what was playing. It was so bizarre to be more than a hundred miles from the nearest community, huddled in a little cabin with a reclusive gold miner as Mount McKinley and the Alaska Range towered over us through the big front window, and listen to a TV audio track of "Charlie's Angels." The dried spruce logs burning in the stove occasionally would crack and pop, and a sled dog outside might howl and yip in the cold air as we listened intently to the story-line and tried to imagine the video action. Of course I'd seen the Angels a couple of times as a kid, and I remembered just enough to know that there were a couple of knock-out blondes with big, uh, hair (like Farrah Fawcett) bouncing around some sun-soaked beach, saving the common citizenry from one thing or another. Looking back on it now, it was a strange scene!

As fall stretched out toward winter, my life in the Bush began to take on the habits of routine. Time spent tending to the dogs and the trapline was punctuated by the regular visits to the Hawk's Nest to resupply, and I was slowly discovering the rhythm of the Alaskan wilderness that had enchanted me since I was a child. The month of December flew by, and as the holidays approached, Dan and Berta extended an invitation to have Christmas dinner at their cabin. I was excited by the opportunity to share trapline stories and found myself really looking forward to the upcoming holiday. I looked at my calendar and carefully planned my trapline workweek so that I would be back at the Hawk's Nest on Christmas Eve. I also needed to allow enough time to put together the only thing I had sufficient confidence to cook as a holiday offering—a rhubarb cobbler. In years gone by, I had learned from my older sister how to cook a delicious apple or peach cobbler, and having all the necessary ingredients except the peaches or apples, I simply planned on substituting rhubarb.

December 24 is an extremely short day at our latitude, with the sun just barely peaking up over the horizon for three or four hours and then fading back down again, leaving most of the day in a listless, dull twilight. That didn't dim my spirits as I found myself mushing my dogs through stands of timber, up and over rolling hills, singing Christmas carols at the top of my lungs, and occasionally sneaking a glimpse of Mount McKinley when the trail broke out into a clearing.

Planning my assault on "Project Cobbler," I arrived with the team in a soft winter's dusk at the Hawk's Nest, then painstakingly prepared my holiday dessert offering for the next day's Christmas dinner. I also took a birdbath in front of the stove where I heated some water, washed some clothes, and picked out my finest, festive, go-to-meeting wardrobe for a wilderness holiday dinner.

Late the next morning I hitched the dogs to the sled for our easy one-mile journey to Dan and Berta's cabin. Since it was just a short little trip, I did not have my normal survival gear stowed in the sled. My only freight was the rhubarb cobbler, which I had nested and tied to the bottom of the sled basket, and a pair of wooden snowshoes, which were fastened on the inside of the basket. You can never predict what might happen out on the trail—and you might just end up having to walk—so like the spare tire we keep in the trunks of our cars, it's always best to have a pair of snowshoes in your sled.

I pulled the hook, and off we went.

It was really just a hiccup for the dogs to Dan and Berta's, traveling on mostly flat and even trail. I could've just as well hooked up a small team of four or five dogs for this little hop, but it had always been my habit to take all thirteen dogs with me—wherever I went. Of course, this is like driving a turbocharged Dodge Viper to visit friends two doors down, but hey, I was dedicated to my team—even if we *were* ridiculously overpowered. Hickory, my young prodigy, was eagerly leading the way running loose in front of my leaders, as his usual spot riding in the sled was now occupied by the cobbler. Thinking back, I probably had close to 700 pounds of husky power at my beck and call to simply haul me, all dressed up for Christmas dinner, and a rhubarb cobbler only a couple of minutes down the trail.

On previous trips to their cabin, I had often checked and cleaned Dan's traps. This is a common courtesy in the North (if you are the friend of a trapper) to check and take any game out of their traps,

Simon, 1989 watercolor.

Simon was one of Jeff's first "real" sled dogs. Here he is taking a break near Wonder Lake.

put the furbearer in your sled, and hand-deliver them to the trapper. In the severe cold of winter, a marten will quickly die in the trap and freeze, and the ever-active mice, the bane of all trappers, will quickly find and chew (and destroy) the pelt in short order.

While on my weekly trips up to Hawk's Nest I had removed several frozen marten from Dan's traps and delivered them. Undoubtedly he would have found the same marten within the next day as he made his rounds, but just a day often will make the difference between a perfect pelt and one with rodent damage—and that translates into more money paid by the fur buyer. On occasion, Dan had returned the favor and picked up my marten as well.

In addition to setting traps for marten, Dan had some traps set up to catch wolf. Normally he would make these sets near his marten traps, simply because it was easier. When he stopped his snowmachine to make his marten set, it was convenient to make one for a wolf nearby as well. However, to successfully lay out and construct a wolf set requires more effort, clever, and skill than a marten set. Marten are curious and fairly easy to catch, but a wolf is quite clever. The credentials and reputation of a trapper are quickly confirmed by others if he catches wolves. And although wolves were common in our area, to my knowledge Dan had never caught one. I suspect he took the time it takes to make the wolf sets as a challenge rather than a way to make a living. I had seen Dan's wolf sets adjacent to his marten traps on many of my travels that winter.

I hadn't even reached the first chorus to my Christmas carol when suddenly, the turbocharger kicked in. The team accelerated into a full-out sprint down the trail that had me frantically grasping for the sled's handlebar in a desperate attempt to keep from having the runners pulled out from under me.

No question about it, sled dogs have a turbocharger, and regardless of which direction they hear or smell something interesting, they will instantly accelerate down the trail at their maximum speed and power. It is completely instinctive and uncontrollable, and you know immediately that they've sensed something. It could be a moose running off the trail to your left, a hare bolting across the trail on the right, an owl swooping low overhead, or anything else moving in the dark shadows that will activate their ancient hunting instincts.

After regaining my balance, I jammed on the brake to try and slow the team and wondered, *What the . . . ?* Just then as we passed over a slight rise in the trail, I saw the source of the dog's wild surge: It was a wolf, twice as big as any of my huskies, caught in Dan's trap and struggling right at the trail's edge. And here was my team of sled dogs, rockin' and rollin' at full speed, completely oblivious to any danger that might lie ahead as they charged down the trail to get to that wolf.

Now most of the time I can control my dogs with voice commands. Usually I'm capable of directing my leaders and team through some of the most intricate patchwork of intersecting paths and trails with subtle verbal commands to go right or left. In fact, I just might be able to write my name in script on a snow-covered lake when my leaders are intently listening to my commands of *gee* for "right" and *haw* for "left." In this case, however, I had about as much control over my dogs as I did the wolf. And that was absolutely none. My entire team was intent on one thing—getting to the wolf.

Typically my sled dogs are hard to slow down anytime, but since they had gone less than a mile and had not even started to breathe hard, my team had absolutely no intention of stopping. The bugles were blowing "Charge!" in their minds. They had no idea what was going to happen, nor had they considered the consequences, but they knew one thing for sure—this was very exciting and that was good enough for them. Compounding matters, I was traveling extremely light—practically no ballast whatsoever. At the top of my lungs I was screaming, "WHOA, WHOA, STOP, WHOA!" and finally accepted that the dogs weren't hearing anything that had to do with slowing down.

Usually you can stop a dog team with a combination of the verbal command "Whoa" and the hard application of the sled's brake to really get their attention. But when desperate times call for desperate measures, there is a last resort. You can't do it often—because there's a likely chance that you will break equipment and definitely put both yourself and your team in a very awkward and dangerous position.

But then, this was a desperate time if there ever was one.

I tipped the sled over sideways and sprawled on top of it,

hoping that the friction of the sled dragging crossways in the trail would stop the team. Chunks of snow were flying everywhere and . . . there went my culinary masterpiece, leaving a delicious streak of rhubarb cobbler spewed on the snow, marking my path as we headed straight for the wolf in Dan's trap.

The tips of my snowshoes, which probably weren't tied in as well as they should have been, were now sticking out of the sled basket. In an instant, they were snapped in half as we careened down the trail. The team's power curve was still revving up at redline as they continued to drag my sled unabated across the hard-packed path.

As I looked up I could see we were less than 50 yards from the snarling wolf and closing fast. I realized that stopping wasn't an option. My only chance was to get the dogs so excited that they might just blow right past the wolf in their enthusiasm. So I jumped off and flipped the sled upright on its runners, releasing any resistance that the dogs might be feeling. I jumped back on and yelled a command the dogs had heard a thousand times, "On by! On by!" hoping we would streak right by Dan's wolf.

It didn't work.

Instead, when my crew of thirteen reached the wolf, they stopped and gathered into a tight semi-circle around their quarry. I was able to brake the sled before it ran into them, and there they strutted like a bunch of back-street hoodlums. Clearly they understood that the wolf was in a compromised situation. All of their survival and hunting instincts hardwired from thousands of years ago erupted in an unrestrained display of ear-numbing barking. Animals instinctively understand when another is in a helpless situation, and the law of the tundra mandates that they try to kill it. In turn, the wolf was aggressively snarling and growling in an intimidating display to keep them at bay. I remember those big jaws repeatedly opening and closing with a loud snap of his teeth, barely out of reach of my dogs.

During this entire episode, I was making some noise of my own, hollering at my dogs, "Leave that wolf alone!" And when they did not listen, I hollered at the wolf, "You leave my dogs alone!" The wolf didn't listen either. My dogs were skirting the edge of their semi-circle—not sure of their next move, but ready for anything.

Dan, that lucky guy, had finally caught his wolf. Unfortunately I now had a job to do, and that was to quickly dispatch the wolf before my prized dog team did something really stupid. Normally I carry a gun, but I didn't that day, so I frantically looked around us for something I could use to complete the task. My eyes caught the marten trap perched on the spruce pole, but it wasn't the trap that interested me—it was the spruce pole itself. Quickly I grabbed the pole, broke it loose from its frozen mooring, and swung it over my head in a menacing Neanderthal war dance. I was hoping to intimidate my team into submission or, at the very least, distract them. But I had forgotten about the attached marten trap, which now flew through the air above me in wide, clanging arcs at the end of the spruce pole. It made my weapon almost impossible to control. I felt like a medieval knight flailing a mace as I attempted to separate my dogs from the wolf.

All attempts were futile.

Okay. Go to Plan B. I took a deep breath, turned to the snarling wolf and used the marten pole like a baseball bat to quickly dispatch him with a heavy blow to the forehead. The wolf collapsed, lifeless. Simultaneously, in a strange twist of canine behavior, the dogs instantly lost interest and stopped barking. They seemed to be thinking, "Oh, that was fun. Are we going on to Christmas dinner now?" To the dogs the entire episode was over. Their attention, now diverted from the wolf, returned once again to getting down the trail. I quickly set the snow hook, steadied the team, and tried to catch my breath as I reflected on what just happened.

Last Light, 1997 oil.

Backlighting enhances the mystical spirit of the wolf.

For me, this had been a momentous event, and I judged that I had done the right thing, under the circumstances. As I gathered my senses, I thought, *Well, heck, I'm no more than a half-mile from Dan's cabin. I might as well take the wolf to Dan's place, as there's no way I can salvage my cobbler that's scattered back on the trail.* I was sure that Dan was ultimately going to be pleased. Putting myself in Dan's position, living miles out in the wilderness trying to make a living, this would be a much sweeter gift for him than my pie. So I heaved the wolf into my sled, pulled the hook, and whistled the dogs up the trail while trying to anticipate Dan's reaction.

That big wolf probably weighed over a hundred pounds and noticeably loaded down the sled as we approached Dan and Berta's. When we caught sight of their cabin, their four dogs started barking like the ultimate doorbell that they were. Clearly, nobody was coming to visit without these guys sounding the alarm.

Well, Dan and Berta were excited to see me and the team, given it was Christmas Day and all. They rushed out of the house waving a greeting as we came down off a rolling hill leading into their yard. Their four dogs ran up the trail to share in the welcome.

I was still a little jittery from the adventure a half-mile up the trail and sang out, "Dan, I have something special for you!" He lackadaisically replied, "Oh, Jeff, did I get another marten?"

"Well, not exactly," I responded as I knowingly leaned against my handlebow.

Dan sauntered up to the sled and casually peered over the side and into the basket. We both were jolted to attention when, at that very moment, the wolf groggily lifted his head—like a heavyweight boxer getting up from the canvas—and scanned his surroundings, looking at Dan, then me, and finally at the dogs. He was down, but certainly not out.

Dan must have thought I was really trying to make this a memorable Christmas.

He nearly bowled over Berta as he ran to the house like an Olympic sprinter. I wasn't sure if he was getting a gun or a clean pair of pants, but I gave him the benefit of the doubt. In less time than it takes to say Carl Lewis, Dan was back on the scene with a handgun and unhesitatingly finished off the wolf, literally, in my sled. We spent that Christmas afternoon properly skinning out and preparing the pelt to be sure it would remain pristine and retain its full value. After our duties were done with Dan's first wolf, we finally sat down and had the wonderful Christmas trapline dinner that I had dreamt about since I was a little boy.

JOE'S NOTES

Trapping in Alaska is a long tradition and has economically sustained many Bush villages. Presently trapping is managed by the Alaska Department of Fish and Game. The wolf, which has aroused emotions in recent years, is still governed by published Trapping and Hunting regulations and can be legally taken in many areas of Alaska with traps or firearms. Go to the Fish and Game Web site to review the state's hunting and trapping regulations at http://www.adfg.state.ak.us.

CHAPTER FOUR
Cracking the Whip

D o you remember the first time you "soloed" in the family car? How about the first meal you cooked for your spouse? (Barbecued chicken on a campfire for me.) As repetitive as a lot of activities become, it's hard to cut through the fog of routine and recall your "first," but I'll certainly never forget my very first dogsled race.

Within a couple of years of my arrival in Alaska I had assembled my first dog team. "Assembled" might be stretching things a bit—cobbling together thirteen dogs might be more accurate, as I now look at that process from my rearview mirror. Nonetheless, I did have a team to work with. I also spent much of my free time exploring the lay of the land encompassing the huge expanse of Mount McKinley National Park. The reach of absolute and unadulterated wilderness out here is almost incomprehensible, and as a result, my long-cherished dream of spending a winter in the untamed wilderness, living the life of a trapper working with a dog team, was coming together.

So after working almost straight through the summer of 1979,

I had earned the freedom to take some time off and had decided
to spend those months in the heart of the Alaskan winter. It was
a remote area that was rich in game, and it fit perfectly with my
criteria for a trapline.

I had done my homework throughout that summer, and in
late October I took my truck over the Denali Park road to cache
my winter's worth of supplies and dog food close to Wonder
Lake. Shortly after that supply run, as if on cue, the fall snow-
storms predictably shut down the road and buried everything
in a thick, white blanket. Almost immediately, I drove my dogs
on the snow-covered road to the north end of the Park and set
up what we would call home for the next several months. From
time to time, I would mush back to Wonder Lake and retrieve
more supplies from my cache and bring them back to restock our
camp. I spent these glorious months out in the Kantishna country with thirteen dogs and lived in a wall tent for the months of
November, December, and January, completely alone, completely
self-sufficient, and completely happy.

It was a unique experience, and the myriad of situations you
face alone in the Bush with only your dogs to occupy your time
is, without doubt, the best teacher for an aspiring dog musher. I
was immersed in taking care of my team, and as a result I began
to really understand what it takes to communicate—and lead a
team—especially one that is accustomed to a life of working. I
learned how to make it fun for both them and me. There is nothing wrong with a hard-day's work—particularly when you get to
do it in the Alaska wilderness—and I noticed that it wasn't long
before the dogs were infected by my enthusiasm. I felt like Henry
David Thoreau reincarnated—it was a great time to think and
meditate and ponder my future, a truly memorable and matur-
ing experience. The self-assured mettle that welded itself onto my
identity that winter has no doubt helped guide me through the
many predicaments I've had to face throughout my life.

I broke camp with my team in late January under some brutally cold temperatures, warmed by a growing sense of self-confidence forged from knowing that I could both handle myself and my dogs in the remote Bush, alone. We traveled more than 90 miles back toward civilization, stopping one night en route. I slept inside an abandoned bus, now better known as bus No. 142, which Christopher McCandless would make famous with his death in the story retold in Jon Krakauer's bestseller, *Into the Wild*. Days later the team and I emerged back at the east side of the Park—an area now known as McKinley Village. This same region has now been expansively developed by the tourist industry to accommodate our huge summer influx of park visitors. The area is hemmed in by hotels, restaurants, and souvenir shops. However, at the time, it consisted of a few sturdy log cabins haphazardly laid out in a rough grid.

Among these aging building was a tavern, long since burned down, named "Paul's Healy Roadhouse." It served, among other things, as kind of an Alaskan version of a community center. There were always notices stapled up on its bulletin board for things to swap or sell, who was coming to town, when the party was, etc., etc.—sort of a pioneer version of MySpace. When I finally "surfaced" from working my trapline, one of the first things I did was to go to the post office to check on my mail. As I passed by the roadhouse, my attention was drawn to a notice on their community bulletin board advertising a sled dog race. It included all the pertinent information regarding the start time, the route, the distance, and how to sign up for the race.

Well, this is cool, I thought. My competitive instincts, which had been hibernating since I had arrived in Alaska several years ago, were rousing themselves from their long slumber, although I don't think I yet realized it. *Let's see, I have a dog team, we've been out working on the trapline for three months, so surely they're in pretty good shape, I know I've got them trained—maybe I should enter*. Not

First Trip, 1988 watercolor.

*Brothers Singer and Simon posed in harness on their first trip to Wonder Lake.
These pups became an integral part of Jeff's racing team in the early 1980s, accompanying him to Nome in 1981.*

only was I having this one-sided conversation with myself, but I was also getting my four-footed sled-dog companions involved in a new adventure without their input. I wasn't certain what their level of commitment would be, but I sure knew that I was rarin' to give it a go. I found myself intently studying the instructions on how to sign up for the race, and then noticed when the start date was. I only had a week to prepare.

So I signed us up and entered the first race of my life—right there at Paul's Healy Roadhouse. With just a week to go, my mind started working overtime on what I needed to do to get ready. The one item at the top of my list was to figure out how to get my team some more top-end speed. I knew my guys had the endurance. After all, we had spent three long, hard months hauling gear and breaking trail out on the trapline. But speed . . . well, to get that I needed some help, and my first thought was to go visit and talk it over with my friend, "Legs."

Legs, as you can imagine, was a tall, towering man that vaguely reminded me of a moose—in that, yeah, he had a body, but you could hardly see it for his legs. Now, Legs was originally from Colorado where he had spent the better part of his life as a cowboy—he still talked the talk and walked the walk. Heck, he was so bowlegged from those many years riding horses that he couldn't sit in an armchair— he just ended up straddling it.

Legs had brought his cowboy mementos with him and they were all proudly on display in and around his little log cabin. I had been coming to his cabin for a couple of years, so I had many chances to closely examine his trophies. Hanging on one of his walls were a pair of shiny spurs, his old weather-beaten cowboy hat, a dark, sweat-stained saddle, and a big, old, coiled-up bull- whip, which really caught my eye. That bullwhip had to be at least 8 feet long, and it was tickling my imagination right now.

I headed over to his cabin and knocked on his door. Legs was glad to see me after being gone for those months on the trapline, and we spent some time catching up. He was interested in my upcoming plans for the spring, and I was glad he asked because, really, that's all I wanted to talk about.

"Legs," I told him, confidentially, "there's a big sled-dog race starting over at Paul's next week, and I'm thinking about signing up."

A true cowboy, Legs was at the ready to help his friend out the best he could. "I'm right behind you, Jeff. You've got a dog team, darn sure, and they're in shape to do it. Heck, yeah, you should enter." He said just what I wanted to hear.

"Well, Legs," I began—he was kind of my sounding board, even though he was a cowboy at his core and probably didn't know much about racing sled dogs—"I don't know much about this racing game."

"Neither do I, Jeff, but if there is any way I can help, I will. You just tell me what I can do." Legs was a straight shooter, a pragmatist, and a man of his word. Having told Legs about my plan, it looked like I was committed to race at Paul's Healey Roadhouse that next week.

As I sat there talking to Legs about this upcoming sled-dog race and lamenting my team's lack of apparent speed, from time to time my eyes wandered to that wall where his memorabilia was on display. The only sled-dog race I had ever seen growing up in northern California was on TV, with Sergeant Preston giving a little shot of encouragement to King and his mighty team of huskies with an impressive snap of a "you know what." I kept stealing glances past Legs at that wall, hoping he wouldn't notice.

"Legs . . . " (we were still in the middle of the conversation about the upcoming race, and I was kind of distracted.) "Legs," I began again, "I think . . . Wow, is that a real bullwhip on the wall?!" (Like I'd just noticed it—I had only been studying that bullwhip for a couple of years.)

"Why, yes sir, that is a bullwhip," said the old cowboy, "An 8-foot, multi-plaited, dual-belly, braided leather thong terminating in a 16-inch fall—it's even got a popper on the end. You know, I used that pretty regularly moving cattle in Colorado." He looked at me, waiting for exactly what he knew I would say next. He was definitely a cowboy.

"Do you think you could teach me how to use that thing?" I asked. I admit that I was under the influence of my visions of Sergeant Preston, but then again, it just seemed poor planning to pass up this once-in-a-lifetime opportunity to learn the skill and art of cracking an 8-foot bullwhip from a master like Legs.

So there began my education in the use of a bullwhip. Legs took the worn, brown leather bullwhip from the wall, inspected the final strand at the end of the whip which actually makes the pop (aptly named the "popper"), and was instantly transported back in time when he was in the business of moving some nasty range cattle. He came to, and we went outside for an introductory lesson on the proper use of the bullwhip and, most importantly, how to make that supersonic, "Let's find a new gear" gunshot "pop" of a true dogsled driver.

I spent quite a bit of time at Legs' place learning how to make that big bullwhip an extension of my arm. First, according to Legs' instructions, I had to let the whip completely roll out behind me, pointing my thumb at the trailing popper. Then in one familiar overhead motion, I threw my arm forward and abruptly stopped with a strong snap of the wrist. It wasn't long before I was consistently creating thunderous "claps" over my imaginary charging huskies.

My real dogs, meanwhile, were resting peacefully back at my homestead, and completely oblivious of my new racing tool. How this would work (in conjunction with the other great theories I was developing) in our monumental race remained a big question. As it turned out, I got pretty busy getting wrapped up in all the other details of race preparation and didn't *actually* make the time to practice the bullwhip with the dogs. *Mere details*, I figured. The bullwhip would be my secret afterburner. It seemed like such a great idea. And practicing with the dogs? Heck, part of the secret had to be the element of surprise, I rationalized.

The week quickly passed, and I soon found myself at the race's staging area at Paul's with about fifteen other teams who were assembled for the race. Dogs everywhere were screaming, howling, barking, hammering their harnesses to get going—just basically freaking out of their minds to run. My dogs, fresh off the trapline, were absolutely bewildered in the midst of all of the excitement. There were more dogs in one place than they had seen in all of their lives, and besides, they were accustomed to going to work everyday on the trapline. In the woods, it was bad manners to bark—I had trained them to be quiet in camp and not send the surrounding game out of the Kantishna. We woke up and went to work every day. They looked at me wide-eyed, like, "What's the big deal? What's with all the commotion? Why are we here? Why are all these dogs barking? Is there something here you haven't told us about, Boss?"

The race at Paul's was a down-home style event, including some classic Alaskan innovations. The start line was simply a couple of spruce poles stuck in the snow at odd angles with a precariously hung, hand-scrawled banner that read "Start/Finish" with the word "Finish" kind of smashed together at the end. It wasn't a particularly cold afternoon, but most of the spectators and race participants were adorned in unlaced, U.S. Army issue arctic Bunny boots, fur ruffs on their parkas, and clasping cold beers in their mittened hands. The official timer had only his wristwatch to calculate the run times for each team. We all pretty much knew each other, and I received several hearty thumps on the back as I was welcomed into the fraternity of racing dog mushers. Of course, there was a favorite to win. I admit I glanced at her with a twinge of envy.

To be honest, my dogs looked like a herd of scared deer caught in the headlights of an oncoming train. As I was hooking up the team, I was could not help but have second thoughts about this racing thing, and really started to wonder if the dogs were even going to run.

My turn on the start list finally arrived. All the teams went out of the start chute at two-minute intervals, so at the end of the race, the times of each team would all be adjusted and the final standings would be announced. The official at the start chute waved to me to bring my team up to the start, and at his instruction, I stopped when the nose of my sled was at the starting line—with my dog team lined out onto the beckoning trail. I silently hoped that the beer-drinking guy in charge of the wristwatch was pretty good at math. As my start time approached T-minus-ten seconds, he did the standard mushing start and counted down from ten . . . "Three, two, one . . . GO!"

And I'll be darned if—after all of my pre-race worrying—my dogs didn't just take off like a dragster fueled with Red Bull. They exploded down the trail at a full lope in hot pursuit of a trophy—I had *never* seen them go this fast! They were pumped up by all the teams in front of them and the fresh scent of dogs on the hard-packed race trail. I was barely hanging on to this little borrowed race sled, as my dogs charged along on the twisting, undulating trail chasing down several dozen dogs they'd just met in a parking lot a few minutes earlier. One thing kept going through my mind, and even though it was an important part of my first time, pre-race strategy, I had to repeat to myself, "I am *not* touching that bullwhip." I certainly didn't need to go any faster—I could barely hang on as it was.

Now, I knew that we were in a race, but compared to working the trapline, my dogs acted like they were on vacation. For them this was easy pulling, the little race sled felt as light as a feather as compared to the sturdy, heavy freight sled they were used to hauling around. And this trail, well, it was if they were prepared to run the rugged, unimproved Baja, and found themselves on the smooth, banked Autobahn instead.

We were gliding through the woods while powering through a few heart-pounding, crack-the-whip type curves on the groomed trail, and we were actually catching and passing other teams. The little racing sled that I had borrowed was initially a challenge to handle on the hard trail, but as the race progressed, I started to relax and found that I could balance the sled on the inside runner and take the corners at full speed. I decided then and there that I needed to get one of these Speedy Gonzales rigs of my own if I was going to enter another race—it was so light and flexible compared to the freight sled I had used for my work on the trapline. I had this revelation, a familiar competitive spirit I hadn't felt for a couple of years: "We might do all right in this race!"

I looked down into the sled bag, and there coiled in a nice loop, sitting on top of my race essentials, was Legs' 8-foot bullwhip. Just staring at me, not saying a word. I tried to resist the temptation. *No way, Jeff, you're going fast enough as it is. These dogs don't need any more encouragement.* I had given myself some good advice there, but there was this other voice inside me that was whispering that this was a sport that fit my physical and emotional profile perfectly—lightweight, athletic, likes outdoors, likes animals, and is extremely competitive. Maybe, just maybe. I looked longingly down at the whip once more.

About 15 miles into this 17-mile race, it was apparent that my dogs still had a lot of steam left. We'd been on the trail for a little more than an hour when it emerged out of the woods onto Otto Lake, where we would then encounter some open, treeless tundra for the last couple miles of the race. For my team of trail-hardened Alaskan huskies, a couple of miles was nothing more than a nice little jaunt—it wouldn't be long before we'd be back to Paul's Roadhouse for a recovery snack, some water, and a cold beer. The trail was awesome, and my dogs must have thought that this light, little racing sled they were pulling was a joke.

The ride across Otto Lake can be beautiful, with the view of

Four-on Four-off, 1988 watercolor.

This is a Yukon Quest Commemorative print. This image illustrates the traditional racing schedule of running four hours and resting four hours. Singer and Simon nap during the four hours off.

Mount Healy and Mount Dora in the background. But I wasn't looking at the view as we came out of the woods and dropped off the trail to make our approach onto the lake. I was looking at the bottom of my sled bag. And I was also feeling this little rush that I hadn't experienced since college, playing football. That competitive part of me was reminding me it wasn't just about winning, but it was also about winning in *style*!

The team and I burst down onto Otto Lake at a full lope. As the trail opened up on the lake, about 200 yards ahead of us I could make out what looked to be an old wooden chair with a cardboard sign resting on it. As is customary in most sled-dog races, the organizers had placed a sign which read "Race Finish 2 Miles," to give all of the competitors a heads-up that now would be a good time to call up the dogs, so as to cross the finish at a full-out sprint.

They obviously had me and my team specifically in mind when they put out that sign. I was racing, my dogs were just steamrolling down the trail, and in one short afternoon, I had found my calling as an Alaskan sled-dog racer. You could say I was living in the moment.

So throwing caution to the wind, I reached into the bag and pulled out Legs' whip. I let it balance in my right hand and felt how its leather-wrapped handle just naturally fell into place across my palm. Wow, did it feel *good*. "Well, I haven't tried this thing out yet—and I am running out of trail. Although the dogs still have plenty of power, and I've passed a lot of teams, I wonder if a sprint to the finish might just be a good idea?" I was trying to consider all the angles of my race strategy in an objective, logical way, bouncing the whip in my hand, when that subjective, emotional voice just drowned everything out: *Darn it, we're running in a race, and we are going for it!*

So, with my left hand holding onto the sled's handlebar, I threaded my right hand through the whip handle's strap and uncoiled that big, old bullwhip to let its full 8 feet of length slither out behind me. I could hear Legs' advice from our brief training sessions, "Jeff, you gotta get it out there behind you—nice and straight—to make this bullwhip do its job and give you the kind of crack you want." And I knew what I wanted. A big crack—not any wussy .22-caliber gunshot-type pop. I wanted a cannon blast!

Out on the lake was nice, open county with no brush or trees to interfere. Indiana Jones would have been proud of me, the way I was setting this up. The dogs were at a full lope, leaning in their harnesses and in the home stretch. My bullwhip was laid out behind me like an arctic anaconda, furiously slithering in the snow. I was crouched on the runners of the sled, one hand stabilizing myself on the handlebar, the other stretched behind me to get the full reach of the whip extended out on the trail. Wow, what a perfect time to crack that whip . . .

Just as I began to snap the whip forward, I felt a violent sensation of something trying to forcefully jerk me off the sled. I instinctively grabbed onto the sled's handlebar tighter with my left hand, as I continued to bring my now heavier whip-laden right hand forward. For an instant I was spread-eagle. I desperately looked behind to see what was going on. It was immediately apparent: Legs' bullwhip had wrapped itself around that chair with the cardboard sign, and was hanging on to one of the legs like a starving python at a pygmy buffet. The dogs were digging in trying to maintain their speed when that old wooden chair suddenly popped out of its mooring and came flying over my head, where it tumbled and splintered into the snow alongside my sprinting dogs. The team surged ahead, wondering what had gotten into me.

Now this wasn't *exactly* what I was expecting while I was spending all that time under Legs' tutelage. I looked around to see if anybody was watching, and although I thought I heard some laughing, I didn't see anybody. I later suspected that the chuckles must have been Sergeant Preston and Indiana Jones. I reeled in that bullwhip and quickly stuffed it back into my sled. As we headed back across the lake toward the finish line at Paul's, I made a quick mental note to hang that whip back onto its resting spot on the wall at Legs' cabin— where it rightfully belonged.

Later that day, the team and I collected our second-place trophy—a pretty good showing for my first sled-dog race.

For the next twenty-five years, as I've continued to race sled dogs, I've never once had the urge to ask Legs if I could use his bullwhip again. I quickly figured out that I really don't need a whip to motivate the incredible Alaskan husky. Give them the right conditions, and they will run like the wind on their own.

Over the years, I figured I've easily covered more than 150,000 miles in races and in training behind a team of dogs. Although the miles have tended to run together over time, there is one constant that I learned from my first race that stays with me even today. And, no, it isn't to leave the bullwhip at home. It is the simple fact that it truly is a blessing that I've been invited and allowed to ride along with an incalculable number of Husky Homestead teammates in countless races over the years. I've been incredibly fortunate to be a passenger and witness to some of the best that my canine friends have had to offer.

Joe's Notes

Sergeant Preston's use of the bullwhip was good TV imagery. In truth, the bullwhip was used historically and commonly as a signal in many early sled-dog races in the North. The early freighters to the gold mine fields used big strings of twenty to twenty-six freight dogs, each weighing seventy to eighty pounds. Those dog drivers popped a bullwhip as part of their signature. The bottom line, it's fun to crack a whip, and I freely admit I have spent time practicing using one to get that consistent "pop."

The question for most people is: Did anyone use the whip to strike the dogs? Probably there were unrepentant jerks who used the whips for punishment. It certainly is not accepted by the general mushing community and precisely why, in the early days of the Iditarod, there were strict prohibitions, resulting in disqualification, against contacting the dogs with a whip. The bullwhip, by the rules, could only be used as a signal.

By the early 1980s, the use of signal whips was not allowed by the rules in the Iditarod. Other races followed suit, and today's races universally disallow the use of signal whips.

CHAPTER FIVE

Breath of Life

very mile of the trail has a story, and this story happened
many years ago on the Yukon Quest trail. It seemed so
unbelievable that it was years before I told the details to
nearly anyone outside my family—because frankly, I didn't think
anybody would believe me. As I write, it has been twenty-five
years, and although I can now freely share this story, it is still a
strong emotional memory. The experience left me changed.

The Yukon Quest follows a 1,000-mile trail between Fairbanks
(Alaska) and Whitehorse (in Canada's Yukon Territory). Early
Klondikers used this trail from Whitehorse to Pelly Crossing,
to the Stewart River, then over King Solomon's Dome to the
Yukon River at Dawson. In terms of competition, most mushers
regard the Quest as the second-most prestigious race—behind
the better-known Iditarod. It's a complete test of the sled dog and
musher, requiring hard pulling over long distances and steep terrain, and also requires speed when the trail is hard and fast. It's a
tough race over demanding country, it's often extremely cold, and

you travel on primitive trails broken out only at race time. As a physical test, mushers give it five stars.

The Quest has only nine checkpoints along the entire 1,000-mile trail, unlike the Iditarod, which has twenty-two. This means the distances between checkpoints are dramatically longer. The longest distance between any two checkpoints in this race is the 230-mile stretch from Pelly Crossing over King Solomon's Dome to Dawson.

Normally, with checkpoints 50 to 60 miles apart, you can just carry a snack in the sled for the dogs and get to the next checkpoint where you have dog food cached for a big meal. But you can't go 230 miles over two days with just a snack. You have to carry all the food and gear necessary to make meals for you and your dogs.

Previously, I had placed fourth, third, and second in this race. I had an eye on winning and thought I could do it 1987. There were a couple of other guys in the race with a similar record who had the same idea. One of them was a Scotsman named Ric Atkinson—a great guy and a fierce competitor who was known for bold moves to the front of the race. He had worked with some huge Greenland sled dogs in the Antarctic in conjunction with a British research team, and then later moved to Canada so that he could learn more about distance racing with the smaller, faster Alaskan husky.

Since I had participated in the first running of the Yukon Quest in 1984, and every one since then, I had gained practical experience about long wilderness travel even beyond my time spent on the trapline. For one thing, I learned that a twelve-dog team of championship-quality Alaskan huskies requires nearly 10,000 calories per dog, per day. At a minimum, I wanted to carry at least two hundred pounds of meat and supplement with some high-energy, kibbled dog food. That means the weight in the sled would dramatically increase, and conversely, the speed of the dogs would dramatically decrease. With loads that totaled more than three hundred pounds, not including the musher, the race becomes a pulling event, as opposed to a running event.

I was in the lead of the Yukon Quest in 1987 after three tough days of racing. A big storm was blowing in and dumping snow on the trail just as I was starting to climb King Solomon's Dome, an imposing landmark of the Klondike.

My team and I left Pelly Crossing on the upper headwaters of the Yukon River at 1,870-feet elevation with everything we needed for the 230-mile traverse to Dawson. I had packed extra dog food for every contingency, including a storm that could slow us down to a crawl. No one was going to help me out if we had trouble, and I knew that self-sufficiency was my responsibility. It's a fine line between racing with enough supplies and racing conservatively. My strategy on the Yukon Quest—even if the extra weight were to slow me down—is to always have enough dog food.

A little more than halfway between Pelly Crossing and Dawson, I was ascending the imposing King Solomon's Dome at 3,800 feet. It was an exhilarating, but physically challenging, section of trail. The wind was howling as the team and I continued to steadily climb and approach the summit. I had a pretty good lead on my competitors and was still able to follow the trail through the trees, but as I broke out of the tree line on top of the Dome, the wind was really sailing. It was snowing hard and the trail was blown in completely. Wooden markers left by the trailbreakers—now barely visible in the ground storm—were the only indication of a trail.

I had been on this trail three times and knew that the exposed summit was only about 4 miles long. If all went well, I would soon be back in the protection of the trees where I was confident that I would find a firm trail again. I wanted to keep my lead. I figured it would be worth my while to use my snowshoes and break trail to get over the Dome.

Snowshoeing is not easy, especially in deep snow and a

Alaskan Blues, 1991 watercolor.

The blue eyes of huskies are magnetic. Here Babe Ruth and Todd show off handsomely. Tommy's eyes add the finishing touch.

blizzard. Even though the dogs can see a hint of a trail, they need firm, packed surface under their feet to pull a loaded sled. The dogs were floundering in the soft, windblown powder snow and were no longer able to break the trail themselves.

Like so many times on my training runs on the Yanert River, I knew it was time to strap on my snowshoes—something most sled dogs rarely see anymore. You have to tell the dogs to stay put while you walk onward ahead of them. For an untrained team, this is incredibly difficult because they don't like to see you walking away—they want to stay right on your heels and follow. That can be a real mess, because the leaders will step on the tails of your snowshoes, sometimes causing you to stumble in the deep snow. The team dogs, in their enthusiasm to follow, will often ball up with the pair of dogs to the front and tangle the tug lines. In a race setting, when you are tired and trying to work through a difficult situation, it can be a wreck in progress. Well-trained dogs that can maintain their positions and wait for the command to advance on the broken trail are the product of a lot of pre-race training.

Fortunately, this wasn't abnormal for my outfit—because we had spent a lot of time exploring in Denali. I had broken trail in front of them on many occasions, so I wasn't particularly worried about my dogs in this situation. Still it's a job to keep twelve anxious dogs under control on a strange trail in a blizzard that's doing its darnedest to blow you over.

With my snowshoes on, I walked to the front of the team. I told them "Stay" as I proceeded, looking back over my shoulder at the team. They barked at my departure, looking anxious to follow. The further I got away from them, the more they were concerned about not being with me, but they continued to obey the "Stay" command. At about 100 yards, they could hardly stand it anymore. I gave the dogs a loud whistle, and they hit their harness, pulling the riderless sled to catch up with me on the freshly snowshoed trail. When they arrived, I said "Stay" and again turned to walk ahead on snowshoes. This gave them a chance to catch their breath. Even though I had broken out a trail, this was not easy pulling. They were waddling in seemingly bottomless snow— and they were not wearing snowshoes. I walked another hundred yards ahead and started the drill all over.

By now we were approaching the summit of King Solomon's Dome, and we were in the full force of the wind. Most mushers will tell you there's nothing quite as unrelenting and unforgiving as the wind. Every instinct inside you and the dogs says, "Boys, it would be a really good idea to get out of this." I was snow-shoeing at an extremely slow pace compared to the team's speed climbing uphill in the trees, where the trail was better. With the blowing snow and the noise of the wind, the top of the Dome was a surreal place—another world. The dogs and I were focused on one thing: to get up and over the mountain and back into the relative protection of the trees on the other side. I whistled for the dogs and they pulled the sled up to me again. I was breathing hard and beginning to perspire in the subzero storm. Heavy frost and ice coated my mustache and eyebrows. Snowshoeing uphill is the ultimate hill-climber workout.

After a half-hour of working hard, just near the summit, I knew the mushers behind us would have the advantage of my trail-breaking efforts.

Sure enough, I looked back and saw Ric Atkinson emerge from the trees below. He was rapidly gaining on us. He was rid-ing the runners of his sled—and clearly benefiting from the trail we'd just made.

He quickly caught up. That was okay. I knew it was going to happen. I didn't begrudge him at all. The up side for me was I also knew him well enough that I expected he would offer to take his turn snowshoeing the trail. This climb over the Dome could take a while, and no one person would be expected to do it all. Besides, two people can work together and go faster. It would benefit both of us to distance ourselves from the competition and worry about our own battle later.

The wind was screaming when he joined us just below the summit. We were okay, but uncomfortable and vulnerable in this position on top of the mountain. I just wanted to get back down in the trees where we could travel in relative protection again. The treeless, wind-hammered top of King Solomon's Dome was no place for human or sled dog.

"Ric, I'll go one more round!" I screamed into the wind. It was understood I would snowshoe for another hundred-yard rotation. Then he could take his turn while I rested.

I left Ric with the two teams and I kept on breaking trail with my snowshoes. Ric came ahead of his team to stand on the brake of my sled. There's a lot of excitement with two teams close together. It's a huge job to keep control of both. You must make sure the towline and tug lines don't get tangled. The idea would be to let my team go once I got a hundred yards out, and his team would then follow just behind. If everything went according to plan, my team would struggle ahead and Ric would then let his team pass, and jump on the runners of his sled as it went by. That way he could use his brake and keep his team from overrunning my team.

The wind was screaming as loud as a jet engine. I couldn't hear a thing, and the blowing snow crystals were hitting me like a sand blaster. When I had gone my hundred yards in the wind and deep snow, I looked behind to see if my dogs and Ric were catching up.

Instead of seeing the dog teams moving, I saw Ric in the middle of my stopped team, kneeling among my dogs, his arms swinging frantically. If you didn't know Ric like I did, you might have thought he was beating a dog. It was so strange, and I had no idea what was happening, but obviously something was really wrong.

I turned around and tried to run with my snowshoes on the new trail. As I approached, I could see Ric furiously waving his arms, scolding my dogs with wild, threatening gestures.

By the time I got to Ric, he was motionless and kneeling in the middle of the team. He had hold of the main towline and with all of his strength he was pulling it together to create some slack. In the middle of his outstretched arms was my dog, Tommy, strangled within a loop of the main cable-filled rope.

Somehow in the confusion of the deep snow, a loop had formed, and in one of those unexplainable events of chance, Tommy's neck had been caught in the noose. Ric was straining with all of his might against the force of the team—which was lunging against their harnesses trying to get up the trail. His face pointed skyward, pinched and distorted with his grand effort. He looked like Atlas trying to hold up the world.

Normally, the incredible enthusiasm of the Alaskan husky is seen as a miracle. They are phenomenal athletes, but sometimes they can be a royal pain, and this was one of those times. All but one of my dogs had a single thing on their minds, and that was getting off King Solomon's Dome. They were bowed into the harness, and I am sure they were thinking, "Jeff is going to be so proud of us; we're pulling so hard to get off this mountain." Unfortunately, I could not communicate to them that they were strangling their teammate, Tommy.

Ric was in a terrible predicament because he was no match for the strength of my dogs. The wind was howling. The snow was blowing. The dogs were out of their minds, barking and pulling, and Tommy was in a chokehold.

That's how I found Ric when I arrived: Looking up at the sky, oblivious to the wind and the blowing snow, he was struggling to save my dog. Quickly I realized what had to be done. Neither of us spoke a word.

I grabbed the towline in front of Tommy, pulling it toward him as Ric did the same from behind. Together we produced enough slack so that we could release the noose from around his neck.

Tommy fell to the snow motionless and limp, eyes closed, his

King Solomon's Dome, 1995 watercolor.

Commemorative print for the Yukon Quest. This dramatic and challenging part of the Yukon Quest trail inspired Donna to interpret the experience in a painting, which has now become a well-recognized artistic symbol of the Yukon Quest. A dependable, determined leader is essential to traverse this section of trail.

blue tongue flopped fully extended out of his mouth. I thought certainly he was dead. Our desperate situation in a driving windstorm on top King Solomon's Dome now seemed insignificant. Tommy was lying lifeless. My competitive spirit evaporated. My dog was dead.

I had never had a fatality. I only knew from others how it might feel.

However Ric never missed a beat. He immediately grabbed Tommy and opened his mouth to check the airway, then quickly closed the dog's mouth. Cupping his hands around Tommy's nose, he started blowing forcibly through his fingers. I was spellbound. I had only heard of CPR for dogs.

I watched as he expanded the dog's chest cavity with explosive lung-fuls of life-saving air. He continued for several minutes— until he was exhausted. I watched in quiet disbelief.

Ric was now out of breath. Gulping for air, he handed me Tommy's head, which lay limp and heavy in my hands. My dog's eyes were gently closed. I was sure Tommy was gone. The wind continued hammering us with driving snow. We could not have chosen a more exposed location for an accident. Ric looked at me with tears in his eyes and said, "I think we lost him." The race, our instinct for survival in the windstorm, everything was forgotten while we held Tommy.

I'll never forget those words of Ric's: "I think we've lost him." I was speechless. He voluntarily shared the responsibility and loss of my dog. To him, we both had lost him. As Ric regained his strength, he repeated his efforts at canine CPR. I thought it was hopeless. I remember whispering, "Tommy, Tommy." In my mind, I was giving him his last rites. Helplessly I watched and tears filled my eyes. "Tommy," I sobbed.

Then, as if by magic, Tommy's elongated, bluish tongue slowly began to slither back into his mouth like a snake on a hot rock recovering from a cold night. Ric saw it, too, and kept blowing with renewed effort. Then my dog's eyes blinked open—looking straight up. Ric was out of breath again, and handed me Tommy's head, still heavy and listless. His body was limp with no muscle tone.

But his eyes were open now and his tongue was back in his mouth. He started to slowly look around and then fixed his gaze upon me. Amazed, I turned to Ric and uttered what we both were thinking, "No one will ever believe us." He slowly shook his head in agreement. It seemed we were witness to a miracle. Too suspicious to believe it could be true, I continued to kneel, wide-eyed and slack-jawed. Slowly a distant smile crept across my frozen, tear-spattered face.

Tommy, my super dog, looked to be operating on a little different and not quite so emotional level. In his regular life Tommy would certainly have been a nightmare as a family pet. Even after a hundred-mile run, when normal dogs would just want to quietly lie down, Tommy would roll in the snow, bounce back up, and start barking for food. Now as he looked up at me with his blank eyes, he appeared to be saying, "What the heck happened, Boss? Are we still in the race? When do we eat?"

I carefully loaded Tommy into the sled bag just as other mushers were emerging out of the tree line and easily catching up to us using the trail we had broken. One of them, Kathy Swenson, arrived and yelled, "What's going on—do you guys need help? What's the hold-up? Get out of the trail if you're going to stop."

It's definitely not good manners to stop in the trail with other mushers behind. But it was obvious that we had been snowshoeing, so she added, "Do you need me to take a turn?"

Over the roar of the wind, Ric shouted to me again, "They won't believe what just happened!" I agreed and hollered back to Kathy, "Hold your horses, I have to load a dog in the sled!" She probably thought Tommy was tired and needed a ride. It's not uncommon to give a dog a ride, and it was just too complicated to explain to her what had really happened.

Ric passed and his team took the lead. Now cresting the summit, we could see the trail again. The unrelenting wind actually had swept the trail clean at the upper reaches of the Dome. It was again shallow enough that the dogs could pull the sled on their own. Fortunately, we were done snowshoeing, and it looked like we were going to get off the mountain. And Tommy looked like he was going to remain among the living.

With Tommy riding in the sled, I followed Ric's team. Even though we could move ahead without breaking trail for the dogs, Ric's team was still working hard in the last of the loose, deep snow and was still not going very fast.

I let Ric and his team get ahead a little, then released my dogs to catch up. Then I stopped again and his dogs continued. We repeated this three or four times, and each time we caught up, Ric looked over his shoulder to see if Tommy was still all right.

All right? Within minutes Tommy was a fully revived passenger, barking like a maniac and attempting to destroy my sled bag. Ric hollered back, repeating what we'd both said on the Dome: "They'll never believe us!" I knew that Ric shared my relief in knowing that Tommy's life-threatening accident was behind us.

As I tried to keep Tommy contained in the sled, he was ridiculously unmanageable, and for him that meant he was back to normal. He had forgotten all about being dead only twenty minutes before. I argued with myself. *Should I put him back in the team?* It was clearly what he wanted. Like a pestering teenager, his requests were wearing me down.

"What the heck," I relented, "let's give it a try." Back in the team, he started pulling as if being nearly strangled to death was a forgotten inconvenience.

As I replayed the events of the accident over and over in my mind, the image of Ric, my competitor, holding my dog's head in his hands, with eyes glistening with sorrow, kept flashing before me. His words echoed the connection he felt. "I think we've lost him." To this day the memory sends a chill through my core, and has left me with speechless respect for this man.

Tommy went on to finish the race as a key member of my 1987 Yukon Quest third-place team. And in the process, he taught me a valuable lesson—one I needed to learn before I could really enjoy winning races. I had been so competitive that I had overlooked how much I appreciated the individual characters of the team. Of course my dogs were my buddies, but once I started really thinking about the dogs as miracles, I started to realize that I was just lucky to be invited along with them for the ride.

Joe's Notes

Jeff ran the very first Yukon Quest in 1984 and persisted annually until he won it in 1989. Tommy's drama on the high slopes of King Solomon's Dome is a look at the complicated relationship of top mushers and their dogs. While no one can explain it in absolute terms, it's clear to the mushing world that awe and respect is one important key to winning races—and Jeff King has the edge. Year after year, armed with an unusual confidence, his huskies continue to perform at a championship level.

CHAPTER SIX

Another Day at the Office

One of the most common questions from summer visitors to our Denali Park homestead is, "Jeff, what happens if you fall off the sled?" It is a legitimate, intelligent question, and I am going to take the time to tell you what I know about falling off sleds.

The answer to this question is exactly what you're thinking it might be. If the musher falls off the sled, for whatever reason—a big bump in the trail, a sharp, icy corner, a low-hanging branch—the dogs will continue to run down the trail pulling the sled without you. Don't hold it against them. I don't. These dogs have not been selected because they are good at *whoaing*. They've been selected because they are good at *going*!

If it happens to you (and it will), you first make a mad grab for the sled as it pulls away from you, generally just out of reach. Then you earnestly put on a burst of speed in a futile attempt to run and catch the disappearing sled and team. You alternately swear like a sailor and plead like an adolescent, while you quickly begin to sweat in your high-tech clothing that was designed to keep an inactive person warm at -30°F. And then, finally, you walk. Sometimes a very long way. And you think, a lot.

This scenario is somewhere in the 99 percent certainty range. The dogs will have known you fell off, but they truly don't care. It is a brutal reality. I wish I could tell you differently—that these beautiful Alaskan huskies I have happily living in my dog yard are so in love with dear ol' Jeff that they will just shut down their engines and screech to a halt if I fall off the boat. They are good-natured, gregarious animals that love to see me coming into the dog yard. But the reality is that running is more important in their world than Jeff. They fully expect me to hang on if I want to come along with them.

Back in the mid-1980s, I was in a great, two-day sled-dog event called the Bull's Eye–Angel Creek Race, which was held during the last weekend of January. I was going to use this race as a tune-up for my Yukon Quest team, since the Quest would begin in the middle of February. The 1,000-mile Quest was my primary focus for that year; still, I enjoyed other shorter races like the Bull's Eye–Angel Creek. And the fact of the matter is, my dogs and I just plain love to race.

Many of my competitors are relatively conservative about their race schedules each season, keeping their eyes focused on the big races. I, too, remain very focused, I assure you, but I rarely pass up an opportunity to race. Plus, I select the dogs for my teams on the basis of their enthusiasm for racing.

These shorter events are great training experiences for my dogs as well as an opportunity to pick up a little prize money to pay for dog food and expenses. At that point in our lives, we were having a bit of trouble making ends meet, so earning a little prize money was certainly an added draw. The Bull's Eye–Angel Creek Race provided an added bonus for me and my team, because we could acquaint ourselves with this 60-mile segment of trail that would also be used for the upcoming Yukon Quest. In addition,

Angel Creek Lodge is a Yukon Quest checkpoint, about 80 miles from Fairbanks, so it was a great opportunity to familiarize the dogs with at least one checkpoint and part of the trail.

The trail started at the Bull's Eye Bar on Chena Hot Springs Road just outside of Fairbanks, and went over hill 'n' dale through black spruce and tundra for 60 miles to the Angel Creek Lodge. The two-day race is typical of those you will find on about any weekend throughout the winter in Alaska. Unlike the Iditarod or the Yukon Quest, where we are racing for ten days straight in wilderness conditions, the Bull's Eye–Angel Creek Race is definitely more civilized. It typically takes about four and a half hours for the winner to cover the 60 miles. Once we reach Angel Creek Lodge, the mushers and their traveling entourage and family just relax and settle in for the night in accommodations with heat, water, and a bed—a luxury compared to racing the Yukon Quest or Iditarod.

Stage Two starts the next morning at Angel Creek Lodge and backtracks the same trail to the Bull's Eye Bar and the finish line. The times from the two stages are added to determine the winner. This makes for some added excitement on day two because each team has the opportunity to take all the marbles back from the winner of the first stage. Notice that a bar is strategically placed at each end of the race trail—an added attraction for those who like to socialize. The event is designed so that mushers and spectators can have an enjoyable, low-pressure weekend—assuming of course, that everything goes right.

We showed up early Saturday morning at the Bull's Eye Bar, signed our name to the race list, got the dogs out of the dog boxes, and picketed them around the truck. I have eyebolts attached to the body of the truck and a few on the front and back bumper. We clip the dogs with short chains to the eyebolts. It's a good system that lets the dogs stretch out after riding in the boxes. At the same time, I know I have control of the situation and know my dogs are secure and safe if I decide to walk away for a moment. It's kind of like letting the kids out of their car seats to stretch a bit and get some fresh air at a highway rest stop.

I discovered that we were one of seventeen teams that had shown up that morning for the race. Typically these weekend races are set up the same way. You amble into the barroom and there, amid the stale air reminiscent of all of the previous evenings of indulgence, a local volunteer at a card table takes your entry fee of fifty bucks and signs you up. The locals and organizers of the race wander in and out of the barroom, and in a short time you gather essential information about the trail and a mental list of the main competitors. About two hours before the start time, the organizers and Race Marshal call for a meeting with all the mushers to discuss the rules and any interesting developments along the race trail while sipping a Bloody Mary. Traditionally, the highlight of the musher meeting is a drawing to determine start positions. Each musher draws a numbered poker-chip out of a well-worn, ragged, beaver hat. (That is, a hat made of beaver fur. Beaver do not wear hats.)

Mathematically it doesn't make a difference where you start. Each musher and team starts at two-minute intervals and, at the end of the day, all the times reflect an adjustment. It is quite possible that the first team to arrive at the first day's finish at Angel Creek Lodge will not be the day's winner. A musher starting further back in the start order conceivably could be the fastest on strictly a time-elapsed calculation. However, depending on conditions, most of us agree the starting order does have some advantages and disadvantages. For example, a fresh snowfall on a race trail may mean the mushers in the early starting order are laying down a trail for the back mushers. On the other hand, starting last might be a disadvantage on a good trail because a good team will invariably have to pass other teams—and sometimes that can be time-consuming. So it all depends, but in my opinion, it doesn't make that much of a difference. The best team usually wins.

That particular morning at the Bull's Eye Bar, I drew number seventeen, which meant that I would go out thirty-two minutes after the departure of team number one. With seventeen teams, it also meant that I was going to be the caboose on this train of mushers racing to the Angel Creek Lodge. Still, it really was not a big deal, because the times were all going to be adjusted.

The trail leaves the Bull's Eye parking lot and runs in the ditch along Chena Hot Springs Road for a quarter of a mile before making a 90-degree turn to cross the road, then continues about 8 more miles to another road crossing. At both road crossings, the trail intersects a major blacktop road with potential for significant traffic. Volunteers were in place to stop traffic as needed and help guide mushers and teams safely across the road. The trail then continues in the woods for another 52 miles and finally ends at the Angel Creek Lodge.

My fourteen-dog team was incredibly excited and fired-up. The rules did not specify a dog limit, so theoretically I could have taken a really huge team—like twenty. That is considered just about the limit of a musher's capacity to handle and, that day, not very practical.

However, the race officials did say at our musher meeting that there were some nasty glare-ice sections of trail between the two road crossings, and for safety reasons they advised no one take more than twelve dogs. Since I was preparing to run the Quest in about two weeks, with a team of fourteen dogs in my starting line-up, I humbly thought, *Ah, I can handle fourteen today. I'll take my whole Yukon Quest outfit. It'll be a great tune-up for the dogs. If everybody else can do it with twelve, I sure ought to be able to do it with my fourteen.*

The more important consideration for me, however, was that my team had to anxiously wait and watch all the other teams depart ahead of them. My dogs are hard-wired to run, and watching another team go out just arouses all kinds of their genetic potential. Not only do they have to watch each team leave the start chute, but the process repeats itself every two minutes and builds a crescendo of frenzied energy.

My huskies saw the first team take off and they were already going ballistic: *There they go! Is it our turn to leave next?* Then another team took off. Frantic with anxiety, my dogs were thinking, *Oh my gosh, surely it's our turn to take off; everybody is leaving but us,* followed by more barking, lunging, whining, and uncontrolled exuberance. With each successive departure of a team, my dogs became crazed and more certain that they were born to do only one thing—and that was to run, now.

When I tell this story, someone always asks, "Why can't you just train the dogs to stay, be quiet, and stand still?" Well, I think I could do that. I have confidence that I could train dogs to do just exactly that, but it would be with different dogs—Labradors or Border collies—but then that would be like entering the Kentucky Derby with a ranch quarter horse that's safe for the kids to ride, instead of a world-class thoroughbred. Basically, we don't select that type of dog for our racing team. Our dogs are a special combination of exuberance and physical capability that allows them to be the ultimate long-distance traveling animal on earth. Mentally they are always driven to run. Sometimes that's a problem, but usually it is just exactly what we want.

At this point, in anticipation of our imminent departure, I had the dogs picketed around the truck. They could bark and express themselves, but they weren't going to get into any trouble. As the starting teams departed to team number ten, however, I started harnessing my dogs and clipping them on to the towline. Of course, once they are in harness and in front of the sled, the dogs are thinking they are about to go any moment, and they get even more berserk (if that is possible). As is typical, the team was securely anchored to the front bumper of the truck with a snow hook. (Although it's designed to dig into the snow like a boat

Sammy, 1987 watercolor.

Sammy is one of Jeff's leaders from the 1980s. This image illustrations the power, speed, and enthusiasm of the Alaskan husky.

anchor, it's also handy for securing the sled and team to trees, trucks, parking-lot posts, and just about anything that's solid.)

The truck was rocking and bouncing as the dogs hammered their harnesses. Fourteen dogs in front of the sled adds up to more than 700 pounds of conditioned and explosive power. Of course, they were not going anywhere yet, but they were trying, and there was a general sense that things could get out of hand once we took the snow hook off the bumper. Finally, team number sixteen bolted off the start line, and it was our turn to advance to the starting chute.

Once my dogs started moving to the start line, they stopped barking and concentrated on pulling as furiously as possible. My standard practice is to stand on the sled brake, cantilevering against the handlebow, with all my might and have my handlers help lead the team into the start chute. From my truck to the start line, you could see where my brake left a pair of trenches and the handlers' boots left long furrows in the hard-packed snow, as we all did our best to keep the dogs from exploding across the starting line. For the last half-hour, the noise of dogs barking and screaming had made it almost impossible to hear, so I had to yell to my handlers to communicate above the din. But as we departed the start line, a strange, surreal silence engulfed the team. At last the team charged down the trail and displayed some of their intimidating power.

My amped-up dogs left the Bull's Eye Bar full-speed ahead as I neared the first road crossing. There, a large group of volunteers were stopping traffic and directing teams across the road. So far, so good. Everything was going according to plan as my leaders followed the marked trail to the road and proceeded across. The sixteen dog teams in front of us had laid down an obvious scent trail, and I had confidence that my leaders were familiar with the "road crossing" drill.

However, midway across the road, some wires deep in the psyche of my leaders short-circuited and abruptly changed our race strategy. Getting a glimpse down the road we were supposed to cross, the dogs must have thought it looked invitingly like a dragstrip runway built for speed. The temptation for them was too great. They decided, "Jeff, there has been a change of plans," as they suddenly turned off the trail and veered sharply up the wide, asphalt runway. All this happened at 16 mph and in a split second. The crossing guards for the race tried to grab my team as we rocketed by, but they were one step too slow.

In the next instant I found myself behind a dog team traveling on an ice-covered asphalt road with traffic—and their momentum was building like a bobsled in the Olympics. My brake, on ice atop asphalt, was absolutely worthless, and the dogs were finally getting to do what they had been thinking about all morning— which was to set a new Land Speed Record. I pushed on my brake with all my weight. Sparks were flying as tungsten-steel tines cut through the snow and gouged into the asphalt. I was out of control and without an immediate remedy.

Ahead, I could see cars approaching and they could see me. The first vehicle in line was a Mercedes Benz, not a particularly common car here in Alaska. Fortunately, the dogs were traveling in the correct lane. The guy in the Mercedes could tell I was in trouble and thankfully started to slow down. He looked seriously concerned, however, as I approached with my snow hook in one hand, hunting for a place to anchor my runaway team.

Something to anchor my team to, I thought. The Mercedes was slowing as I contemplated where I could hook onto this luxury car that would not get me sent to jail. To him it looked like I was going to implant it somewhere into the front fender. His eyes got as big as saucers as he saw my outstretched arm grasping the ice hook. I am sure this was a new experience for him. The Mercedes screeched to a stop and then into reverse and started to back up at 16 mph. With the car now retreating, my dogs had a new and exciting reason to run. Like all dogs, they love having something to chase. They put it into overdrive to catch themselves a Mercedes Benz.

Lucky for me, Mr. Mercedes could not go far because traffic was coming up on him from behind. He had to stop. Lucky for him, a pickup load of guys that looked like they understood sled dogs burst out of the vehicle behind him like a SWAT team and grabbed my runaways before we found out if my dogs could pull a Mercedes. These five guys were lifesavers and helped me turn the team around, untangle the dogs, and get pointed back in the right direction toward the road crossing and the trail. A look of pained relief flooded the face of the Mercedes driver.

The dogs were still overly exuberant, but with everyone's help, in an instant I was screaming back down the road, out of control again, but at least toward the intersection of the road and the race trail. When I got there, I would have to make a 90-degree left turn, or I was going to be in big trouble all over again.

Meanwhile the volunteer crew back at the road crossing had watched from afar. It was obvious I was having some big problems. Quickly they implemented an ingenious plan as they saw me coming at them on the return path. They locked arms and formed a human barricade across the road so that the dogs would have essentially *one* option—take a left and get back on the race trail. With eyes squeezed shut and heads turned away, they heroically stood their ground as we approached. Without breaking stride, the dogs curved left and followed the human fence line back on the race trail. At the last moment, several of the volunteers abandoned their posts to dodge me and my sled as we saw-whipped around the tight turn.

Back on the snow-packed trail, my brake worked way better, and I could attempt to calm and focus the team, getting them into the rhythm of the trail. What a way to start a race!

This wrong-way fiasco cost me some time, but now we were back on track. I knew that nobody was behind me, so all I had to do was look ahead and try to reel in some of the competitors. After cruising 4 miles in the next fifteen minutes—and halfway to the next road crossing—it was obvious that the dogs were just warming up and were still in overdrive. Despite all the excitement, they had not forgotten about the sixteen teams who had deserted them earlier at the parking lot.

Recalling that the officials had mentioned a particularly tricky area of ice on this stretch of trail between the road crossings, I tried to talk the dogs down. I do this all the time in training because the tendency of the team is to always travel faster than my strategic plan. This may sound strange, but racing long distances is more about conserving energy than it is about speed. Of course, speed is necessary, but I always want the dogs to run in a comfort zone. Remembering the recommendations of the Race Marshal, I was on the lookout for the rough, icy trail ahead. His warning ran through my head like a Wall Street ticker tape, *You really shouldn't have more than twelve dogs, maximum.*

Boldly I had thought, *Yeah right, what's two more dogs to a pro like me?* That is, until I arrived at this spot, which was glare, polished ice layered in big frozen bulges and angular slabs that looked like a lava flow. It extended in all directions from the trail into the brush and appeared as if an underground spring had sprung a leak and had been building this ice monument all winter. Specifically, we call it "a trail glacier," and it had formed into a bulbous, uneven, treacherous surface. To make matters worse, the markers indicated the trail took a sharp turn.

The dogs were cranked up and doing around 15 mph. Despite the ice and the difficulties it presented for me, the dogs were in pretty good shape as they began to cross because a layer of thick frost gave them reasonable footing. However, this did nothing for the runners of my sled, which had absolutely no traction. I careened and bounced across the ice until the inevitable occurred and I tipped over, desperately hanging on to the handlebar, being dragged and screaming pathetically, "Whoa, whoa!!!" I am sure I looked like Superman flying through the air as I was hanging on in an effort to stay with the team. I knew that they absolutely would not stop.

I always wonder why I even bother to yell "Whoa!" when I know there is no reason that these dogs, excited by speed, will heed my request. People ask me all the time if I can stop the team with a voice command, and my answer never changes. It's always "No." Yet, I still scream "Whoa!" when I lose the team or tip over, dragging. Part of me says, *Jeff, you know they're not going to stop just because you're yelling "Whoa,"* and another part of my brain adds, *They hear you, they know you tipped over, but they just don't care.*

Their only concern was to run and catch up with the rest of the sixteen teams that left for the party earlier in the morning.

They had been taught to run like mad and that, one way or the other, I would stay on the back of the sled.

Ordinarily, if you tip over on snow, the sled on its side will eventually bulldoze a pile of snow in front and accumulate some ballast. The dogs will begin to realize there is something heavy back there and, *hopefully*, come to a stop. On ice, however, the sled pulls just about the same standing up or laying down. Either way, it pulled so easily it was only a minor inconvenience to my dogs, which by then had had more than 2,000 miles of training in all kinds of conditions. My only hope was to hang on to the sled until we got across the ice and back on the snow trail.

Before that happened, however, my head slammed into a trailside spruce tree, and I was knocked loose from the sled. Dazed from the blow, I got to my knees, shaking my head. I remember seeing my team, in perfect formation, screaming off down the trail at race speed. Then the sled, which was whipping from side to side behind the dogs, hit some brush and was bounced back upright just as I caught the last glimpse of my runaway team. It appeared as if a ghost rider was driving the sled.

The next instant, I was reminded of one inconvenient consequence of being musher number seventeen that particular day. There would be no musher coming from behind who might possibly give me a ride on his or her sled. Generally in these circumstances, you would have about a fifty-fifty chance that a musher coming up from behind would give you a lift and ultimately help you catch your team further up the trail. I would always give a ride to a musher who lost his team if I could. It always seems to come out in the wash. Besides, carrying an extra human for a few miles is not that big a deal. Today, however, that option would not be available.

I thought my dilemma through and calculated that the next road crossing was still 3 to 4 miles away. The road-crew volunteers would surely catch my team as it emerged from the woods, riderless.

Now, if you happen to have a Big Shot in your neighborhood

who needs to get chopped down a couple of notches, send him up to me. I'll dress him in the gear it takes to stay warm at -30°F and see how far he gets trying to chase my runaway dog team. This is one of the most humbling experiences imaginable. Mary Decker couldn't catch my dog team in her track gear, much less me wearing the boots and gear required to keep warm at -30°F.

I started to run and immediately recognized the futility of ever catching the team this way. As I shed clothes and slowed to a walk, it soon felt like I was in Texas, sweltering on a hot summer day.

The gear I wear to stay warm at these temperatures makes me look like an oversized pickle, and to illustrate the point, I will divert for a moment to the subject of clothes. It was summertime, and I was in a grocery store in Fairbanks a couple of years ago, doing some necessary shopping for the family, when my "Alaskan celebrity" status got me recognized.

In Alaska, the Iditarod and the Yukon Quest are a big deal, and having won them both, I'm regularly stopped by fans for an autograph or a "Howdy-do." As I was working the aisles, more or less incognito in my summer clothes, I passed a mother and her young son pushing a cart down the cereal aisle in the opposite direction. The little boy looked up at me and did a double take. I heard him whisper, "Mom, that's Jeff King!"

The mother looked directly at me like I was an imposter, then turned to her son and harshly replied, "No, it's not!"

I didn't want to take sides on a mother-son discussion, but I felt I must speak up. "I beg your pardon, Ma'am," I replied, "but, yes, it is."

Shocked, she replied, "You're Jeff King? Really? I didn't recognize you with your clothes on." An awkward pause hung in the air as nearby shoppers looked up, trying to sort out the bizarre exchange of information. Realizing what she had just said, the woman turned bright red and tried to correct herself: "I mean, uh, WITHOUT all of your clothes on."

I tried to rescue her. "Ma'am," I said, "I think you better just stop right there. I know what you mean."

The fact is, she pictured me wearing my bulky winter gear— the way most fans ever see me. The gear that we wear is virtually a portable shelter. We must be prepared to be out in absolutely abysmal weather, sometimes for days at a time. Our gear not only protects us while we travel, but also when we stop and rest. It is one of the big keys to survival.

Back on the trail of the Bulls Eye–Angel Creek disaster, there I was plodding down the trail in my winter gear, totally overdressed for the job of pursuing a runaway dog team. I could only imagine what was happening with my team up ahead as I trudged, step by step, half-baked in -30°F temperatures. My sweaty hair began to freeze, and I was soon moving at an Alaskan snail's pace

Meanwhile, as I discovered later, musher Number Sixteen had been zooming up the trail, suspecting that Jeff King was probably going to gain on him, and he was looking back over his shoulder for the inevitable moment when he would have to stop, yank his sled off the side of the trail, and let me pass. As he looked back, he saw instead a riderless dog team advancing at a blistering pace. I am not sure he would admit it, but I'd bet he let out a little chuckle.

He did, however, do the only responsible thing. He stopped his dog team, essentially blocking the trail. He anchored his snow hook to the base of a black spruce tree nearby, and waited for my dogs to hit the dead end. Although the trail itself was hard-packed, its margins were loose snow nearly 4 feet deep, which prevented my team from just "going around." There was no place to go, and they just piled up like an accordion behind team Number Sixteen. They knew I was gone—but they really just didn't care.

Then musher Number Sixteen did something that's a bit risky. He trusted his snow hook to hold his dogs and went back to unravel my outfit. Normally, the rule is to stay in front of your team or an arm's length from your sled—just in case you have to grab the handlebar if your hook pops loose and the dogs take off. But he proceeded to wade back through the fourteen exuberantly wagging tails of my dogs to get to my sled. He took my snow hook in a similar manner and securely anchored my team to another nearby black spruce. He was losing time for sure, but it was the right thing to do. There are risks to the dogs when the team is running loose, and every musher knows it. So race or no race, any musher worth his salt would do anything he could to help a riderless team, regardless of how it might affect the outcome of his own race. Satisfied that my team was okay, and knowing that he had done his duty, he returned to his team and pulled his own snow hook to get back in the race. He could proceed knowing I owed him a case of beer, or something, and that someday I might do the same thing for him.

As musher Number Sixteen pulled away, he looked back to hail a final "farewell" to my team of screaming banshees anchored to the spruce tree. He took in the view with a sense of satisfaction, then was alarmed to see the tree swaying back and forth with increasing velocity. Determined that they would not be left behind, my team surged ahead, and the 15-foot tree was uprooted from the earth but still stuck to the snow hook. It began dragging down the trail behind the sled. My team had pulled the tree out of the ground and was running again, this time pulling a 15-foot spruce tree.

Oblivious to all of this turmoil, behind them on the trail, I was having my own personal workout as I ran and walked in my many layers of warm clothing, my gigantic boots, and parka.

Back up the trail, musher Number Sixteen was not too happy with my team as they overtook him again, now dragging a tree. *Oh, great*, he was thinking, *I have to stop again and tie up Jeff's maniac dog team. This time I'm gonna pick a bigger tree.* Fortunately for him, the second road crossing was just coming into view, and a new plan developed. He yelled ahead to the volunteers, "Jeff's team is coming, and they're dragging a tree! And Jeff's not with 'em!"

My charging huskies, still dragging a 15-foot spruce pole, exploded after him headlong into the crew of volunteers, where they were engulfed by helping hands. Now, finally, they had some adult supervision—for the first time that morning. Team Number Sixteen continued, zooming ahead, while volunteers swarmed my unruly canines, straightened them out, and anchored them to the bumper of a Ford F150 truck parked on the roadside.

Back on the trail, I was considering the possibility that my Yukon Quest team, the fourteen dogs I had worked so hard to condition for my biggest race of the winter, surely would have been injured. This team was favored to win the race. Surely one of them would have twisted a shoulder, gotten tangled in the towline, or the whole team might just be plain exhausted. My season could be over, and I was sincerely worried about the possible ramifications of my cocky decision.

It took about thirty minutes for me to hoof it to the road crossing. As I approached, I was an overheated, anxiety-ridden sweatball. I could hear the dogs barking in the distance. When I was closer, I was relieved to see my fourteen dogs hooked to the Ford F150, on the verge of pulling it down the road in the wrong direction.

"Are they okay? How many of my dogs are hurt?" I asked the road-crossing volunteers, still sucking air from my cross-country run.

"Hurt?" one guy said, "We can just barely keep them under control! Get back on that sled."

I went from ultimate depression to elation for the third time in less than an hour. I didn't know if my psyche could take too many more misadventures. The volunteers helped point us in the right direction, and a couple of them pulled the ice hook from the bumper of the Ford. I put the ice hook back in place on the handlebar of my sled, and we were off again—literally, to the races—at a 15 mph lope. The temporary rest at the road crossing had given the dogs another chance to get wound up about missing the party further ahead up the trail.

The 15 mph breeze in -30°F reminded me of I how much action I had seen in the last half-hour. I was drenched in sweat, wet through and through, and starting to freeze my tail off as I stood on the back of the sled runners. Although my gear is designed to dry out while I'm wearing it, nevertheless, the evaporative cooling that is driving the moisture away chills you to the bone. We were going too fast for me to jump off and run to warm up, so I just shivered and suffered and gradually dried from the inside out. After a while I warmed up and was back in race mode as we gradually caught and passed many of the teams on the trail to the Angel Creek Bar. I was so relieved to have just made it through the first day race intact that I hardly paid attention to the "day times."

My family and handlers joined me for the night at Angel Creek, and the next morning we left the start line in reverse order, a typical dogsled-race tradition. The slowest team from day one leaves first, followed at two-minute intervals by the faster teams. This is a management trick to help the slower teams get to the finish at about the same time as the winners. It was at that point that I realized that we might still have a chance at winning this race. My attitude changed at the start line of day two, and we charged off once again in pursuit of the winner's trophy. Throughout day two the team and I passed every team that was still in front of us and ultimately were edged in the final tally of times—by just one team. We finished second overall.

In retrospect I have often pondered this near-disaster. It has occurred to me how the mental attitude of the dogs, and a positive "Success is Mandatory" outlook from the musher, continue to surface as two of the most important attributes in dog-racing, and maybe in our lives in general. The dogs' own energy had clearly created some serious challenges for the race when selfish leadership left them virtually unguided. Their energy needed to be "focused on the task." They needed poise and confidence with an emphasis on perspective and direction. With these ingredients, their desire and enthusiasm became a key to success.

Incidentally, I did buy a case of Alaskan Amber for Number Sixteen.

JOE'S NOTES

On average, a championship-quality sled dog weighs in at about fifty-five pounds, where it seems the balance between power, endurance, and lung capacity is ideal. Conditioned and in top shape, a motivated team of fourteen huskies is a formidable bundle of out-of-control biomass when pulling a thirty-five-pound race sled with high-density plastic runners designed to slide with minimal drag. Just to set the record straight, trained huskies in the weight-pulling category for under fifty-five pounds have individually pulled sled with loads approaching twenty-five hundred pounds.

CHAPTER SEVEN
Old Hickory

I'm often asked if I have a favorite dog. My favorite answer is: *That's like asking me if I have a favorite daughter. The answer would vary from day to day!* Surely many of you can relate to this.

However, over the years I have had a few standout dogs that have secured a place in my memory and my heart forever. Some with dynamic personalities, others outstanding athletes, and a few with an uncanny combination of common sense, athletic ability, and a natural determination to get me down the trail. One was a tall, lean, muscular, smoky brown dog with a mental strength that still leaves me in awe. His name was Hickory, and he was my prized leader for many years. But more than that, he was my trail partner and my best friend.

Hickory came into my life in 1979, when I was twenty-three years old and working at the Mount McKinley National Park Station Hotel. Back then the hotel was not much more than a Pullman railcar along the tracks, and it was the only hotel anywhere close to the Park entrance. It was nothing like the complex of restaurants and hotels that exist here today. Then, I was just a young guy trying to make a living and hustling to maintain my thirteen sled dogs through the summer, and keep alive my dream of spending a winter on the trapline with a dog team.

I had heard that a friend of mine had bred a topnotch racing sled dog into her kennel. It was an idle remark in a casual conversation, but I perked up when I heard that some of the pups might be for sale. Even in my earliest days of sled dogs, I knew that genetics were an important part of developing a kennel. Some of the larger, more established kennels were making concerted efforts to improve the performance of the Alaskan husky and keeping detailed records of performance and genetics.

Although the Alaskan husky has never been recognized as a breed by any of the purebred registries like the American Kennel Club, mushers were keeping their own registries and following performance for generations. Some of the legendary names of the mushing world at that time included George Attla and Gareth Wright. They were breeding top dogs from all across North America, and producing phenomenal sled dogs with an ingrained "attitude" to travel and run. Mushers were beginning to realize that the genetic potential of sled dogs was just being discovered.

With the advent of the Iditarod in 1973, long-distance mushers also learned that the raw physical capacity of the Alaskan husky to travel surpassed their wildest imagination. Quickly, the sharp mushers recognized key sled dogs around the state and made certain that the bloodlines of their kennel boasted these genetics. Over the spring and summer, mushers would travel great distances to have their female huskies bred to a great-performing male. It was not uncommon for western Canadians to drive a couple of days to Anchorage or Fairbanks to get in on the action. Since I was just putting together my team of sled dogs, I became fixated on trying to get one of these "race dog" pups.

However, I was broke.

As it happened, around that time, one of the cooks from the "Zoo," the hotel employees' cafeteria, stopped me one day and asked if I wanted several boxes of outdated hamburger patties that were destined for the dumpster. Everyone knew that I had a few extra canine mouths to feed at home (which was a tent on the hillside just north of the park boundary). It was a great resource to hear of the ground beef and a lucky score for a guy like me. I jumped at the chance to supplement my dog food cache. But instead of feeding it to my dogs, I ultimately went over to my friend's place and negotiated what turned out to be the deal of the century. I traded that 100 pounds of bum hamburger for a little male puppy that was advertised as the offspring of the topnotch sled dog I had been hearing so much about.

I had already made extensive plans to take my thirteen dogs up to the northeast boundary of Mount McKinley National Park later in the fall after the tourist season. It had been a childhood dream of mine to set up a trapline, live in a tent, heated with a small sheet metal wood stove, and travel by dog team. However the acquisition of my new pup was complicating my plans, since he would be too small to make the 90-mile trip by dogsled from McKinley Village to the area I was headed. I ended up sending my pup out with some friends of mine, Barb and John Parker, a young couple who were chartering a Bush plane to their remote log cabin on Moose Creek, not far from my proposed campsite. They had agreed to take care of him while I made my way by dog team to their place. Afterward I could then take my new pup in my sled on a short day's run to my trapline camp.

The plan progressed, and I soon drove my team overland on the historic 90-mile trail through the national park out to my friend's hand-hewn log cabin to pick up my beloved puppy. I had named the pup Hickory, for his deep brown color that resembled the wood—the same wood that I'd used to build my first real dogsled. When I arrived, I found that Hickory had quickly adjusted to life in Bush Alaska and was the new playmate for John and Barb's only other pet, a large house cat. The peaceful, solitary life of the cat and my two friends had dramatically changed since the arrival of Hickory.

Their little one-room cabin had a cat door, a major concession to my friend's feline pet. Alaskans pride themselves in having near airtight homes to maximize fuel efficiency, so having an extra door, no matter how small, that opened directly to the outdoors was normally taboo. To counteract this Alaska Bush faux pas, John had hung a moose hide over the entire opening that functioned as a first-class weather stripping.

When I arrived, I was eager to get reacquainted and play with my little pup—he clearly had boundless energy and curiosity. But he totally ignored me. He was in perpetual motion playing hide-and-go-seek with the cat. The cat played the game well and would make a bold exit out the cat door with Hickory in hot pursuit. The cat would push her way out and Hickory would make chase, just narrowly missing the cat as it exited through the flap. Then he would stick his head through to his shoulders and look around outside as the cat then sat smugly out of reach. Hickory clearly had the run of the house and was gaining a confident understanding of humans.

Saying farewell to John, Barb, and the cat—with my new pup tucked safely in my sled—I departed to set up camp with a plan to make a little money trapping the elusive marten. Obviously, Hickory was too small to run in the team, so I carried him in the basket of the sled. Afterward, everywhere I went, Hickory rode just in front of me, and soon he understood that this was his place.

The bigger that Hickory got, the more comfortable he became riding on the sled—like a dog that rides in the car looking through the steering wheel. He became so confident that while we were moving, this charismatic pup would eventually run back and forth covering the entire length of my freight sled (the one I'd made from hickory). In no time, he became even more daring and would jump out of the sled and run alongside until he was tired. Then Hickory would bark and whine and signal for me to stop the sled, and he would jump back in and take a breather while the team took us further up the trail. He was always hoot and became a huge part of my experience that winter.

Once when I was mushing down the trail with Hickory riding in the sled, it appeared as though he were considering being part of the team. With the sled in constant motion while the team was moving over uneven ground, Hickory developed an uncanny sense of balance. Traveling to the front of the sled, he rode as if he were captain of a ship in a storm.

Connected to the front of the sled is the main towline that extends through the team of dogs and each dog's harness is connected to it by a shorter tug line. The force of the dog team moving over uneven trail is concentrated on that single, main towline. It gyrates, bounces, loosens, then tightens and is constantly in motion as the dogs and sled swoosh down the trail.

After a while, Hickory became so good at riding on the front of the sled that he cautiously stretched out one of his front feet to test the towline. First one and then the other. Over the course of several weeks, he continued practicing this balancing act with what I can only refer to as "dogged" determination. He honed this skill until he could effectively ride in my bouncing, sashaying sled with both front feet perched on the bobbing towline while his back feet remained on the sled—like a tightrope walker. He was a source of great entertainment for me—I couldn't wait to see what he would do next.

Hickory's talent eventually progressed even more, until he could ride the towline with his front feet and plant his two back feet on the thin brushbow of the sled—and *still* keep his balance. During his practice sessions, he would occasionally lose purchase and tumble off the side of the sled, only to scramble up out of the snow and come running and whining after us, begging for another try.

When I came in off the trapline later that winter, I entered my first sled-dog race with the same team of thirteen dogs. Although Hickory was leading the team by the end of the trapping season, he still lacked the physical maturity to race. However, a year later, when I entered my first Iditarod in 1981, Hickory was my leader as we departed downtown Anchorage. He was just a year and a half old, and already "Commander-in-Chief." In front of thousands of cheering spectators, he displayed a tremendous amount of canine poise for such a young dog.

It was a long way to Nome that first year, for both Hickory and me. But we cut our "race teeth" together and both became trail-savvy wilderness travelers.

Over the course of the next six years, Hickory grew into an elegant and muscular sled dog, and I became a successful dog-sled racer. In 1987, I raced the famous Susan Butcher in an event staged in the remote Brooks Range. The "Coldfoot Classic" took us through the Gates of the Arctic, a spectacular canyon on the upper reaches of the Koyukuk River guarded by two peaks. From there it seems you can see all the way north across the barren arctic slope of Alaska. One of the most beautiful sites I have ever seen.

Susan Butcher had just won her second Iditarod several weeks before, and was well on her way to becoming a mushing legend. At one point during the 300-mile Coldfoot Classic race, my team caught and passed Susan with Hickory in single lead at the front of the team. Susan was famous for having a keen eye for dogs, and as I went by, she yelled out, "Jeff, where did you get that lead dog?!!" It was a moment I'll never forget, and I swelled with pride as Hickory guided my team down the dicey, icy John River. He had caught the eye of the most famous racer of the time. He got the credit he deserved.

Hickory was with me on the challenging Yukon Quest race during those years, too. Though Hickory was my most trusted leader, he was often *not* put in the lead. It is not uncommon to run your best leader in the middle of the team where they relax—just to enjoy the scenery and trot along with the team. Less-spectacular leaders are chosen for the less-challenging trail, and just like saving your best pitcher for the toughest game of the World Series, Hickory was my "closer."

This was the case in the 1986 Yukon Quest, as we approached Eagle Summit, a notoriously steep section of the trail. I had a good trail leader in the front, but she did not have the same drive, reliability and "head" as Hickory. As we started to climb, the wind began to stiffen, and I was thinking about switching leaders. Many mushers consider the wind as the most formidable weather obstacle, especially when the dogs must run into it face first. The compounded effects of the cold and wind can challenge even the best lead dog's common sense. Windblown snow can collect on the muzzle of the dog, penetrate the undercoat, and sometimes build up around the eyes. It is a challenging test, even for a sled dog bred for arctic conditions. When wind is added to a very difficult climb, a weak-headed leader will start thinking about turning around and heading back downwind—to perceived protection. Hickory had already proven his mettle in many such difficult situations.

By the time we reached the steepest incline, however, it was obvious that I should have changed leaders earlier. We were completely exposed on the mountain, and there simply was not a good place to make a switch. The team was attacking the steep, barren mountain in a bitter, stiff wind. I was pushing the sled from behind to help the dogs in this pure test of strength. Occasionally I would "Whoa" the dogs to give them (and me) a breather. The steep incline required me to stay behind to keep the sled from sliding backward, which made the notion of changing leaders even more unreasonable. As it was, I had to drive my ax into the snow behind a sled runner to keep us in place when we paused for the dogs to suck in some more air. Obviously it was just too

Snacks, 1988 watercolor.

dicey to leave the sled and try to climb forward to my leaders. I reluctantly accepted the fact that I might have screwed up. I could only hope my leader would be tough-headed enough to handle the pressure of our situation.

Suddenly, Zipper, the big, black female I had selected to lead the team, turned her head out of the force of the wind—which was hitting us from our left side and blowing straight downhill at 50 to 60 mph from the left to the right. I imagined what she was thinking, and looking down that mountain, I had an uneasy feeling about what was going to happen next. Zipper snapped, "I have had enough of this wind and I am not going up that trail anymore." She lost her nerve and abruptly turned the team 90 degrees to the right, bolting off the trail down a steep slope.

Almost immediately we were out of control, and I thought we

The team is stopped for a snack, a breather, and a pat. Jeff and Hickory share a moment of mutual respect and affection.

might be cashing it in. There was no way to set an ice hook and the sled brake barely slowed them down. After several hundred yards of pin-balling off various obstacles, careening downhill, I finally managed to stop the sled precariously at a steep gully near the bottom of the near vertical mountain. I struggled through the wind-blown drifts and, crawling on my belly to the front of the team, I got Hickory into the lead and Zipper put back in the team. I felt lucky to be in one piece and figured I must be more conservative about climbing the daunting Eagle Summit. Conservative we would be until the wind died down and we got out of this mess.

I turned Hickory into the wind with voice commands, and we headed back up the steep incline to intersect the trail. We had been in a tough and dangerous situation, but we weren't out of the woods yet. I stopped the team for a moment in a small windbreak formed by drifting snow, and I went up to Hickory. Looking into his face, I said, "Hickory, just get us up this hill to the trail. Once we do that, we'll go back down off the mountain and wait for the wind to die down."

Off he went again, retracing our near-vertical fall to the bottom. When he intersected the trail, Hickory made a command decision to buck into the wind and go in the direction we had originally been traveling when Zipper lost her nerve. It takes tremendous effort for the dogs to pull a load up the steep ascent of Eagle Summit—facing into the wind—and it takes pure confidence and poise on the part of the leader to get their teammates to follow.

I watched Hickory as he led the team up and over Eagle Summit in that howling wind. He drove straight into it, the bulging muscles of his hind legs flexing with each step. He was a marvel, a committed athlete that earned, and deserved, my total respect.

Over the years, as our children grew up, Hickory was often a one-dog team for a toddler. We would put our little three-year-old daughter on the sled, say, "Hike, hike, Hickory!" and off they would go, up the driveway. Hickory also had an innate ability to judge authority and was selective about his job assignments. Donna was often frustrated with Hickory because he usually assumed a blank look of misunderstanding whenever she asked him to do the simplest of commands. I tried to explain to her that Hickory was capable of some very involved tasks. With me driving the sled, he would weave in and out of parked cars, pass teams, turn the team in a wide circle to the right or left, break trail, remember old routes, and never lose his enthusiasm. Most importantly, he was an innovator. If I needed to cross on questionable ice, for example, he would assume responsibility and figure out the best and safest course. I often let him do the thinking, and I was rarely disappointed. It seemed he was a one-man dog.

If asked, he would trot figure-eight patterns in the snow with voice commands, understanding the tone of my voice to indicate the degree of turn I wanted. I had tremendous confidence in Hickory. As I got to know more sled dogs over the years, I appreciated even more his incredible talents.

I remember the time a grizzly bear came into the dog yard, which is situated within view of our house. It is not an everyday event for sure, but it does occur almost every summer at our home in Denali. The bark of the dogs is so different when they see a grizzly bear. It is so distinctive, yet rare, and every time I hear it, I ask myself, "What the heck is that?" It's a bark that is somehow reserved for the King of the Arctic, because no carnivore, not even an annoying black bear, will elicit that strange, choppy yelp from my kennel of dogs. Over time, I have decided that the "grizzly bark" is probably a combination of respect moderated with outright abject fear.

I came out of the house to investigate, "Holy crap, it's a grizzly bear!" The bear was on the edge of the dog yard, pacing back and forth, eyeballing the dogs, and unconcerned about me. Ninety-nine percent of the dogs were pressed back up against the inside of their doghouses like wallpaper.

However, the dog closest to the bear was Hickory, and he was standing on his back legs at the forward end of his chain, fearless, barking as if to say, "Make my day! Just try it, big guy." For a moment I watched Hickory try to take on that bear, willing to do battle. Thank God, he did not. Before the incident was over, I ended up having to shoot that grizzly bear, who went down less than ten feet away from my great lead dog.

It just doesn't seem fair that a dog's life span is so much shorter than ours; that something so special can be born and grow old in such a short period of time.

Old Hic was just over nine years old when I left him in the house on the fateful night of our house fire—January 4, 1989. Hickory was a special dog, one that I trusted implicitly, so much so that on that evening I had decided to leave him in the house, where it was warm and comfortable, before I departed to the neighbors for dinner. When I got the call letting me know about the fire, the first thing I thought of was my dog. *Please, God, some-one get him out of the house.*

No one got there in time.

Hickory's picture hangs in several rooms of our home, and I think of him often—the entertaining puppy, the exceptional leader, and my best friend.

JOE'S NOTES

Hickory was a familiar Alaskan personality leading Jeff's team. I traveled with Jeff on the 1984 Yukon Quest and watched this remarkable animal break trail for many miles. On one occasion, we reached the Alaska–Canada border and were confounded when the trail suddenly stopped at a section of the Yukon known as the Thousand Islands. Steam and fog rose from dangerous, open water and we knew were in a delicate situation. As race leaders, however, a group of us realized we had no option but to put in the trail ourselves. Hickory led our train of teams for many miles across dangerous ice and, in large part, took us to the Canadian side, where we safely rejoined the trail.

CHAPTER EIGHT

Magic Carpet

January 4, 1989, the day Hickory died, was also was my wife's thirty-fourth birthday—a day I will never forget. Donna and our two girls were still on the East Coast visiting her family over the winter holidays. I had flown home early to continue training my team of sled dogs and preparing to run the Yukon Quest in mid-February. The 1,000-mile race from Whitehorse to Fairbanks was again my main focus for the year. It is a tough trail, and I knew that the dogs needed me to get them in condition. To date, my best finish had been second place. I had my eye on winning this time.

Earlier that day, the dogs and I had gone on a long training run. On return, I fed them and got them bedded down on fresh straw in their houses for the night. Knowing that I was "baching" it for a couple of days, my good friends Bruce and Jeralyn had invited me to dinner that evening. Before I left, I had put my two leaders, Hickory and Snickers, in the house. It was cold out, and I'd figured I would give them the executive treatment and let them spend that night with me in the warmth of the house.

I was relaxing at dinner and thought my day was done. But

our dinner was interrupted with a frantic call from my handler, Jim Brown.

"Jeff, your house is on fire! Get home quick!"

Donna and I were nearly finished building our dream home. We had lived in a two-room daylight basement for years as we saved money to build the two-story home over our heads for our growing family. We didn't want to move in to the new section until it was completely finished, and we estimated we were only about a month away from that exciting day. With the help of many good friends, we had hauled every board and pounded every nail. The phone call hit me like a lightning bolt.

I tried to remain under control as I ran from my friend's cabin to my truck, and sped up the Parks Highway with Bruce and Jeralyn in close pursuit. As I drove up our driveway, I could see the windows of the house blazing bright, then dying out as the fire gasped for air. The local fire volunteers were already there struggling to contain the hot interior fire. I was mortified by the thought of my two lead dogs still in the house. I ran past everyone, charging the front door and heaving it open. Thick smoke and heat billowed out the opening as I frantically attempted to find the two most cherished dogs in my small racing team.

"Jeff, it's no use!" screamed Jim, as he pulled me back. "The smoke is too thick. It's been too long. They're gone."

I'm not sure at that moment in time, I could truly understand the impact of the scene. I didn't have the luxury of time to grieve. My mind immediately shifted to the next task at hand—putting out the fire.

It was a long, seemingly endless night, and the memory of it remains with me—vivid and painful. I remember the exhausted and blackened faces of my neighbors, each of whom had dropped everything to come running and help. Every time I looked up, I saw another new face. I don't know how many people were there to help me, but before it was over, it would be most of our community. We finally called the fire "out" the next day and had saved the basic outer structure. Although a building was still standing, it was a disaster inside.

Donna and the girls arrived home two days later. Our friends and neighbors had worked laboriously to clean out the charred debris from the home in subzero temperatures. The house was gutted and reeked from the smell of smoke and fumes. I was in the construction business, and I knew this was not only a huge financial loss, it would be a gigantic project to get the house repaired. It was a long couple of days. Even longer months loomed ahead.

Mother Nature didn't help. The temperatures dropped to as low as -68°F and remained bitterly cold for several weeks. Undaunted, the community organized work parties to begin repairs. They provided meals for all, day care for our girls, and a shoulder to cry on. It was a powerfully charged period in our lives.

All of this happened barely six weeks before I was to strike off from the start line of that year's Quest. My racing career had been gaining momentum, and my hopes were very high for that year's challenge, especially considering what had happened a year earlier, when my race ended abruptly on the very first night of the race.

The previous summer, in August 1987, I had injured my wrist severely in a construction accident. A power saw cut through just about everything important at my left wrist, leaving me with a hand that functioned, but just barely. As a result, my hand was nearly void of sensation, and essentially could not sense warmth, and more importantly, cold.

In the 1988 Quest, I had planned ahead to keep my damaged left hand protected with heat packs inside my mittens. However, the maintenance of my hand got away from me on the brutal first night at -35°F. At the second checkpoint, I was forced to scratch from the race with frozen fingers. It was one of the first big disappointments of my developing racing career.

So, part of my strategy for the 1989 Yukon Quest was to really safeguard my left hand. I obviously could not chance freezing it for a second time—or my racing career really would be over. It was part of my preparation and planning to make 1989 my comeback year. Now, after the fire, it seemed that running the race *at all* was in serious doubt.

I sat down with Donna and talked it over. I felt that it was my obligation to forget about racing and concentrate on repairing our home. However, she was adamant that I should race in February, regardless.

I tried to put the house fire in perspective. No one in my family had been injured or killed. However, Hickory was gone, and that loss cut deep. As you know, he had not only been my lead dog, but he was also a special companion. I often left him in the house so that he would be more comfortable. It was a special perk for a great dog. It is very possible that Hickory had something to do with the fire—we never figured it out. But as a result, my prize leader, who had led the team in so many races and was such an important part of my life, was gone.

Undeniably, I had some tough challenges during the time leading up to the 1989 Yukon Quest. The injured hand, the house fire, and the loss of my leaders were huge blows. Actually it had been a couple of bum years. I realized, however, that it was all a matter of perspective. My wife was philosophical and said, "Jeff, we just need to get through this race. You don't need to try to win this one, just do your best to make this a positive experience. Have fun. Take those dogs out there in honor of Hickory."

With Donna's urging and support, I entered the race in 1989— without my old and trusted friend. It was full speed ahead.

As I prepared to run the big race, I got calls from all over Alaska from people I had never met. The generosity was overwhelming. They began sending all kinds of stuff—clothes for the kids, money for dog food, and in some cases, even offers of sled dogs.

One call was particularly interesting, from a man I barely

knew: "Jeff, I have a great old lead dog that might help you out, and if you need her for the Yukon Quest, we would love to have you use her." In the next couple of weeks I got to know Roger Hocking as well as you'd know your next-door neighbor.

It's unlikely to find a dog a month before the Yukon Quest that has had the training and conditioning to go on a grueling, 1,000-mile race. Ironically, I discovered that Roger's leader was previously owned and run by Joe Runyan, my former competitor and a friend. The dog was a little female named Hickey, who was amazingly similar to my lead dog Hickory. She was almost nine years old, but she had stayed in shape that winter leading a recreational team. I was told that she was a steady little trotter and was good on glare ice, so I thought she might help me out. Hickey was put in the training program just two weeks before the race and seemed to fit well into the team.

Reorganized and determined to run the Yukon Quest, I departed my home in Denali and drove 750 miles to the race start in Whitehorse, Canada. I decided I was just going to have a good time and put the house rebuilding project behind me for now. Per my wife's instructions, I was going to focus on a positive outcome that didn't necessarily need to strive for that elusive win.

It was an emotional moment for me as I stood on the runner tails looking down First Avenue—the Whitehorse street that served as the starting chute. It was lined with hundreds of cheering fans and well-wishers. A month ago I was focused with all my competitive spirit to win this race. Now, I was here with my team, without Hickory, determined to just have fun and use the race as a learning experience for the future. My team was harnessed, the sled was packed, and I was minutes away from the 1,000-mile journey.

Moments before I released the team, the crowd parted and revealed a petite Native woman holding a pair of mittens—handmade moosehide mittens decorated with beautiful embroidery and beadwork. She looked right at me and obviously was coming to talk to me. Shyly she said, "I want you to take these mittens. I made them for my husband, and his hands have never been cold in them. We want you to have them." I knew she was remembering last year, when I had frozen my fingers and was forced to scratch.

Although on my best day, I'm not much of a talker, her generosity and kindness left me completely speechless. I slipped my hands into the beautiful moosehide and stammered an inadequate "Thank you," my mind racing with the significance of her gesture. Those mittens warmed a lot more than my hands. To this day they hang in a very special spot in our home.

The officials at the start line gave me the countdown, and we departed down the streets of Whitehorse hoping to leave the troubles of the last year behind. Bad luck is purported to come in groups, and as I admired my new mittens, I was convinced I would make sure that that bad luck was now behind me.

Over the course of the first couple days of the race, I have to admit things were going well. I was traveling in a pack of the top teams, and my dogs looked at ease and comfortable—they were eating well, sleeping well, in excellent condition, and making good time when we were running on the trail. Though I was competitive, I had relaxed my hallmark focus on scrambling and gaining every second. In many ways, I was just relieved to be on the trail.

As we continued making our way to Dawson City, I realized we had gained some time and were actually maintaining a couple of hours' lead over the competition. And, I realized, I really wasn't trying that hard! I have learned in years since that I actually do better when I am diligent, but relaxed. It is one of those competitive ironies, but I was learning that trying too hard had been keeping me from the winner's circle.

By the time we reached Dawson City on the Yukon River, the team and I had hit our stride and were definitely leading the pack. For practical purposes, Dawson is the midway point of the race, so we had come almost 500 miles through some very rough country and soft trails. The Yukon Quest rules require that the musher take a thirty-six hour break in Dawson—a welcome rest for the mushers and the dogs. It also fits in nicely with the Yukon Quest philosophy: Spectators, families, and friends can help their favorite musher, and we can get fully updated on the first half of the race. Practically speaking, it makes sense for the organization, because the veterinarians can take extra time and look at each dog. The times are adjusted at that point to equalize all the differences from the start times in Whitehorse. If I started twenty minutes behind another musher, for example, my time is mathematically adjusted so that I would leave Dawson with a twenty-minute benefit. Everything was well-organized.

After the thirty-six hour layover, I left Dawson City at -38°F on a crystal-clear night, two hours ahead of my nearest competitor. The clock showed a little after midnight. Once again, my life was like a surprise party. Four days after leaving Whitehorse, thinking myself just lucky just to be on the back of a sled, my team and I were leading the race.

We followed the trail markers onto the Yukon River, where I knew we would travel downstream to the Canada–Alaska border and then on to Eagle, Alaska. This was a long 150-mile segment of wilderness trail. My main concern was the first 30 miles of trail on the big river. I was well aware of the notorious open leads in this section of the Yukon. Minutes after leaving Dawson, I was traveling in fog created by the open water—mist that lies on the river as thick as pea soup. However I could look straight up through the fog and see the stars and the aurora borealis—the green lights flashing through the moonless sky.

The fog was eerie at -38°F—so thick that my headlamp light reflected back off the wall of white. I couldn't see very well, and I knew the fog meant dangerous open water. However, I had faith in the trail crew that had put in and marked the trail. They were dedicated volunteers, knowledgeable outdoorsmen who understood the Yukon in this area. They were capable of finding the good ice and able to avoid the bad. Trail markers—surveyor lathe wrapped with reflective tape—were easy to spot from a distance with my headlight, so I just had to follow one to the other, like the yellow brick road. Still, I stayed extra alert.

Within forty-five minutes of departing Dawson and well on my way down the Yukon River, the fog was dissipating, and we were now out of the area known for open water. I could relax a little.

My scheduled departure time had put me out at midnight and by 2:00 A.M., I was starting to get pretty sleepy. The dogs were just clicking along at a steady trot. The rhythm of their footfalls was like a soothing lullaby. The fog was gone, the trail was in good shape, and I allowed myself to do what I often do in similar situations. I allowed myself to "check out"—that's what I call it: "checking out"—meaning staying just awake enough to avoid letting loose of the sled—but no longer really paying attention. I know the dogs so well, and I let them go on autopilot. My trusted leaders steer the ship.

I actually get some rest doing this. I would be slow to call it sleep, but I am resting. I am not paying attention, but I can feel the sled and the cadence of the dogs, and know we are going the right speed. I was trying to set myself up for the last half of the race—which I knew would be grueling. Every opportunity to relax could pay off later.

There is a trapper's cabin about thirty miles down the Yukon River from Dawson on the south bank, where Cassiar Creek flows into the river, and I was thinking of it as a destination to take a break. It would be a perfect place to get out of this extreme cold. I was hoping that the trapper, who I had gotten to know over the past several races, would be there and have a warm fire blazing in the cabin.

Traveling down the river at 2:00 A.M., half asleep, I was suddenly jolted awake when I felt my dogs surge forward. It was as if a moose had come on the trail and the dogs had broken into a lope to chase it—which happens all the time in the woods. However, it's fairly uncommon to have a moose in the middle of the Yukon River in the middle of the night. I was baffled. It had to be something else.

As the sled lurched forward, I opened my eyes, snapped on my headlight, and realized that just off to my left side was a large black hole of open water, a mere six inches off the trail. The hard-packed ice of the trail was just teetering on the edge of the open lead. The dogs had surged ahead because they also recognized the hazardous combination of bad ice and open water. They had accelerated to get past it.

I stomped on the brakes once we were safely beyond the most apparent danger and tried to gather my thoughts. My next instinct was to give the dogs a command to put on the speed, just like when you're stuck in a snow drift with a car and it's too late to back up—and you feel your only chance is to blast through it. That was my instinct that night. I made a quick decision and commanded, "Hike! Hike! Hike!" The dogs heard the seriousness in my voice and charged forward.

A moment later, I reversed the engines, once again slamming on the brakes and hollering, "Whoa!" On second thought, I'd decided to wait a moment and evaluate the situation. I had just gotten by one very dicey situation, and quickly was realizing that I had just stumbled smack dab into a minefield full of new, very dangerous threats. I slowly turned my head, lighting the area around me in all directions, and detected steaming, open water, shining like a mirror. The scene made me catch my breath as the seriousness of my situation sank in. This was definitely a place that I did not want to be. In evaluating my predicament, I accepted the fact that the cavalry was not going to come to our rescue. There was only one guy who was going to get me out of trouble. And that guy was me.

With my light on, I could see that the now foreboding, heavy fog was back. I looked behind me, and I could see the open water. In front of me, I could see the dogs. They stood with their legs splayed on moving, thin, flexible ice and looked like they were trying to balance on a waterbed. Standing on the runners of my sled, I could see the water seeping into the snow around me, like liquid absorbing into a paper towel.

My dogs were wearing nylon booties. At -38°F below, I am always careful to protect their feet from the abrasiveness of the cold snow. As the water wicked through the snow into the booties, they became saturated and immediately began freezing to the super-cooled ice. The booties were becoming anchored to the surface, complicating an already difficult situation.

The dogs struggled to release their feet—a phenomenon that I had never seen before or since. I knew that it was imperative that I get their booties off. The main concern was the undulating ice. I hoped that it was just a newly formed surface, and that underneath this ice and water was the more substantial, solid ice of the Yukon River that had formed during the winter.

What I am describing, called overflow ice, is not uncommon. During the course of the winter, a thick slab will form on the surface waters of the Yukon. With a couple of -40°F or -50°F cold spells, this surface ice can eventually grow to 4 or even 5 feet thick. Of course, there are tremendous hydrologic forces operating, and sometimes it freezes so thick that it eventually blocks the water channel underneath. This often happens at the mouth of a tributary flowing into the river. Then water is forced up through cracks and fissures, trying to find a release channel, where it escapes and flows out on top of the exposed ice.

While you would think that overflow would be more common in warm weather, the process gets started in very cold weather. That emerging water starts to freeze in the low temperatures. My dogs and I were on top of this newly formed surface over about a foot of flowing water. Beneath it, I hoped, was secure ice. Anyway, that was my theory. It was also possible that these same forces had opened a dark hole of the deep Yukon River. Now that puts a musher's senses on alert in a way that you can't believe. Step into the open water, and you may never find bottom.

Usually I resist the temptation to get overdramatic. Let me just say however, this was the REAL DEAL. I recalled the two mushers I have known who died as a result of falling through the ice with their teams.

I stepped off my sled and walked slightly away to distribute my weight. I knew that the weight of the sled was already starting to disintegrate the ice beneath it. As I moved, I broke through the overflow into knee-deep water. I splashed through the ice and moved along beside my dogs. Their weight alone was not great enough to break the newly formed sheet of overflow ice, yet they were barely supported. I knew if I got too close, they would likewise break through into a foot of water with lots of jagged ice all around them.

At arm's length, I reached out and started to remove the booties of each dog to release their feet from the ice. Each bootie acted like glue when it was wet and had frozen to the new ice. Without their booties, the dogs were unencumbered and free to easily move again. Once I got all of the booties off, I went up to my leaders, Bandit and Babe Ruth.

These two were "autopilot" lead dogs. They were not my best leaders. However, because the trail had been so good, I was saving the best leaders for a more difficult situation.

Well, we were in one now. I missed having Hickory with me, not only for his leadership ability but for his moral support as well. I walked ahead of the team in the darkness and fog to figure out how the heck I was going to get us off this floating waterbed of ice. *Where was some secure and safe trail?* I punched at the overflow ice, carefully evaluating its strength and trying to find a route that was solid enough to hold me. I searched with my light through the dark night and thick fog hoping to find safe passage.

In cold temperatures like these, the ice is forming so fast that in some areas it is solid, yet 2 feet away, it won't hold you up. I wandered around looking for solid ice. Once I found a route that would support me, I put my footprints on the frosty surface so that the dogs would have something visual to follow. The solid ice I did find was not taking me in a straight line—it turned and wandered unpredictably, but it was the best I could do.

With my headlamp I could see the trail markers ahead, and it was obvious that the overflow had built up a couple of feet since the trailbreakers had marked the trail. A few markers were submerged 3 feet deep into the overflow—just the reflective tip of the wooden lathe was visible. Since it was absurd that a trailbreaker on a snowmachine had put the markers in 2 or 3 feet of water, I knew I was caught in the middle of a very recent event. Below-zero temperatures had frozen the Yukon ice so thick that it had choked off the flow of water underneath. Now we were wading through a dangerous sea of frigid water, broken ice, and slush.

As I moved ahead, I spotted a firm snow trail that was unaffected by the overflow water. That was the good news. The bad news was that just before that good trail I could clearly see an open channel of disintegrated ice and flowing water. That flowing water was running perpendicular to the Yukon and had originated from a creek emptying into the river. It was that water that apparently had been plugged by the freezing temperatures, was forced to the top, and was now flowing onto the frozen surface ice.

I could only hope that this 8-foot-wide flow of creek water was running over a solid mass of river ice, which would give solid footing on a crossing. I couldn't be sure, but I knew I had to get the heck off of where I was—and I had no choice but to chance that it would hold us.

I switched my dogs around and put Hickey in the lead, a dog I didn't know that well. But I knew she had a lot of experience running with Joe Runyan's team. I had used her off and on in the lead, and she and I seemed to have a good connection. I respected her experience, and she must have respected mine. I put her head in my hands and said, "Hickey, I really need you. You need to pay attention. This is not good, and nobody is going to be coming along to help us for a couple of hours. This whole thing is going to be done long before that."

Then I did something that I had not done in years. I attached Hickey to the front of the team with a long line. Years before, when hauling gear for climbers to their base camps on Mount McKinley, I would attach a single leader with a long line, up to 8 feet, so he or she would be provided with the freedom to seek out a safe path through the crevasses on the glacier while unencumbered by the following dogs. I needed to rely on Hickey's natural river sense to guide us all through this mess.

I went back to the sled and gave the forward command. I guided Hickey over my footprints using "gee" and "haw" commands. Right, then left—she was listening to me and looking for my footprints on the good ice.

As she came to that open lead, nearly 8 feet of clearly flowing water, she looked back over her shoulder to me. We were at a critical juncture. If Hickey jumped in the water and turned back, the team would likely be tied in a big knot of tangled dogs, and the situation would become even more desperate. I had to be convinced that she was going to make every effort to cross that water and not question my command. After mushing with dogs for thousands of miles, I realized that in a dangerous situation, when you really need the efforts of your dogs, everything was based on trust. Either you have it or you don't. I knew that if she stopped at the edge, it would be very difficult to get the momentum of the team going again. We would be marooned in a lake of overflow.

I called out, "Hickey, hike!"

She got to the water's edge and launched herself like a Labrador retriever going to fetch a downed duck. The power of her

10th Crossing, 1992 watercolor.

This print commemorates the 10th Anniversary of the Yukon Quest, symbolized by the 10th crossing of the Yukon River.

jump pulled the next two dogs into the water—and once committed, those dogs started paddling. I was immediately alarmed to see that they were not touching bottom! I had hoped that the flowing water was not deeper than their legs were long, but it definitely was, and the front of my team was paddling, not running, to the other side.

The next two dogs went in, and I realized that we were now committed. As the next couple of dogs went in the moving water, I started to think, *I hope the water is not so deep that I can't touch the bottom. Surely, there is ice under the water, and even though the dogs can't reach the bottom, I'll be able to touch it.*

It was my only hope. About the time Hickey reached the other side, my sled went into the flowing water. I held onto the sled, feeling for that ice I trusted would be underneath me, but only kept going deeper and deeper until I was fully neck-deep in the ice-cold waters of the Yukon River.

I struggled to keep my sled upright, but it rolled over from the combined pressure of the slush and the moving water. The water immediately rushed in to fill my sled bag and snowsuit. Gasping at the shock of frigid water filling my clothes, I started to work my way to the dogs, grabbing the main towline, and using it like a lifeline. I moved hand over hand toward Hickey at the front of the team. As I did so, I submerged some of the dogs like buoys to hold me up as I went over the top of them to get to the edge of the ice. There I found a crack in the ice, pulled myself up, and then grabbed Hickey, who was floundering at the ice ledge. I hauled her on top of the ice with me and kept pulling. I never stopped moving for a split second.

I was very scared and operating on pure adrenaline as I kept pulling Hickey, and finally the next two dogs were out of the water. Understand that, once out of the water, these dogs were more concerned about drying off than they were about pulling their buddies out of the drink. They were shaking off the water and trying to roll on the ice. I screamed to the dogs "Pay attention!" They had to pull and get the rest of the team out of the open lead.

They leaned into their harnesses and the next two dogs came out of the water, and with each new pair I had more power to pull out the balance of the team. By the time I got the last two dogs on top of the ice, the sled had capsized underwater and the sled bag was filled with slush.

With only a moment to think, I glanced at my left hand. It was still a long way from a complete recovery from that construction injury. I was considering the frostbite damage to my fingers—the reason I scratched from the race a year ago. With almost no feeling—or sensation of cold—in my left hand, I knew I was highly susceptible to refreezing it. Now soaked to the bone, I realized that the dry clothes and the fire starter I had in my sled were going to be the difference between life and death. My liquid methanol fuel and matches were in a waterproof container in my sled bag.

I reached down and tried to pull on the sled, but I could barely move it. The slush was now jamming it to the side of the open lead and building dead weight on the sled. I called to the dogs.

One of the most distinct memories of this incident was the voice that came out of my mouth at that instant—it was a part of me that I had never heard before. It was a guttural, Neanderthal scream to attention. The words were not clear, but the message was unmistakable. "I need your help now! Get up, lean into your harness!"

I started to pull with all my might. The dogs leaned into their harnesses, and like a slowly breeching whale, the sled inched out of the dark hole. Water flowed out of the sled bag into the -40°F night air. As the sled lightened and plopped down on the trail, I immediately went at it, digging through the sled bag. *Was the waterproof bag of clothes and methanol fire starter still there?*

They were.

I aimed the beam of my headlight to the far banks of the

Yukon River. The Yukon was a mile wide in this area, and there was nothing to burn out here—the river's banks were 20 feet high and covered with 3 or 4 feet of powder snow. It would be an incredible effort to climb up to where there was firewood. I looked the dogs over to see if they were okay. Amazingly, they looked almost invigorated—like this close call, this brush with death, and now safety, gave them new life.

They were barking, rolling in the snow, and started to jam their harness in the direction down the trail, which was now clearly in front of us. I quickly decided that climbing the steep bank and looking for firewood was out of the question. It seemed my best bet, with the dogs quite willing to take off again, was to continue down the river and hope for a big pile of driftwood. Oftentimes on the Yukon, driftwood accumulates in piles as big as a house with brush packed in among the logs. I had seen logjam piles in the past where a small flame and a bottle of fuel could turn that woodpile into a bonfire that would make a college frat party envious. I concentrated hard, trying to think myself out of this predicament. There would be little room for error during the next hour.

I grabbed the sled handlebar, gave the command to go, and the team took off like a bullet. While they were running, I was rummaging through my sled trying to reach my dry mittens and spare clothes. Bouncing down the trail, however, the best I could do was change into my dry gloves and mittens. And I was just now starting to really get cold. It had been -38°F when I left Dawson City, and I had no idea what the temperature was on the Yukon ice, but it had to be getting colder.

About twenty minutes went by—and still no pile of driftwood. Usually the driftwood accumulates over the summer on the upriver side of a sandbar or island, but I was rolling the dice that night. The channel was wide with no sandbars or islands in sight.

I was trying to analyze my situation: *How cold, really, was I?*

I needed to be able manipulate my hands enough to strike a match and open a bottle of fire starter. As we were going down the Yukon, I could see that the fog was clearing, visibility was good again, and the stars stood bright in the sky. I remembered one of my favorite poems, "The Cremation of Sam McGee," by Robert Service, about Sam McGee's buddy following Sam's last wish and using the boiler of a derelict steamboat on Lake LeBarge as a crematorium. He tore up floorboards of the *Alice May* and made a huge bonfire before he stuffed in Sam to send him off into the afterlife, warm at last. I ran with that thought and started to envision lighting my sled on fire—the only thing around that might burn.

At the same time, my incredible dogs were really starting to pick it up. We were going over big bumps in the trail and the sled was bouncing off angular slabs of rock hard ice. I was having a heck of a time staying upright as we ran through a long section of ice rubble that had formed when the Yukon froze up earlier in the fall. Looking at my watch, I knew that almost an hour had now gone by since the drenching in the overflow. My outerwear had frozen solid like a suit of armor, barely bending at the joints.

I could wiggle and maneuver my body away from my frozen clothing. I would never experiment on purpose, but I can tell you that as you move inside wet gear that's incrementally freezing, you gradually form fit yourself in an oversized cocoon. The cold was a little more tolerable if my skin was not *actually touching* the frozen interior surface of my suit.

I knew that time was running out and I had to get warm soon. As I was moving down the trail, I tried to calculate how far it was to the trapper cabin at Cassiar Creek. *Where the heck was I?* Remember, I had been half-dozing earlier that morning and really didn't have my bearings. I know the river pretty well, but the fact that I had been dozing—checked out—made it hard to tell exactly which bend of the river I was taking with the team. The

Yukon is immense and some of the bends may take a dog team an hour or more to cover. In that darkness and cold, I could not picture exactly where I was.

I scraped the frost off the face of my timepiece at about an hour and fifteen minutes into this ordeal. I didn't know how much longer I could take it. Still no pile of driftwood, and the thought of burning my sled, a momentary comfort, was absurd. There was no firewood, and I was trying to figure out what to do.

Even when I am tired, I always check my watch and keep a close mental record of my travel times. Time is so illusory and the only way to keep the dogs on a regular schedule of running and eating is to just form a habit of checking your watch. I also like to keep track of time in case I lose the trail. I will usually know, almost to the minute, how long it will take me to retrace my tracks to the last-known location. I was fighting mental fatigue, but I knew we were within fifteen or twenty minutes of the time I thought it would take to get to Cassiar Creek. If I could just hold it together a little longer . . . I struggled to move and create life-saving warmth.

Then the teeniest little light appeared in the distance and affirmed my prediction. It was almost symbolic of how crazy my life had been over the last month and how I had been tested. It was a little yellow glow, and I recognized it as a lantern that had been hung in the window of the trapper's cabin at Cassiar Creek. There is a tradition in the North: If you think there is any possibility of travelers in the night, you hang out a lantern. It says, "We're home. It's warm inside. We may have gone to bed, but don't worry, just come on in and make yourself at home. Put another log on the fire, and we'll see you in the morning."

On this night, the tradition was kept alive by a French Canadian trapper named Cor Guimond. He had run the Yukon Quest before and knew that mushers might be coming through, so he had set a coal oil lamp in the window of his cabin. When my dogs saw the light—they bolted. They understood as well as I that light meant rest and a hot meal. They almost slung me off the back of the sled with their enthusiasm. I hung on for all I was worth, and felt the strength of the team as they loped to the bank of the river that led up to the light and the cabin.

The difficult trail up the bank off the river was a steep 45-degree incline. It appeared too steep for the dogs to pull the weight of the sled and me, so I instinctively jumped off the runners to help push the sled up the slope. I was quickly reminded that I was frozen in a cylinder like the rusted Tin Man. I tipped over, but I hung on to the sled, while the dogs put on a demonstration of power and dragged me up the hill.

When the team pulled up to the cabin, I was very near done in. Through the window, I saw Cor Guimond, his head resting on the table, sound asleep. Shivering, I rummaged through my sled bag and found the bag of ice-covered snacks for the dogs. I stumbled from one dog to another as I gave them each a cold treat of fatty lamb. I would have to wait until I thawed myself out before I could start my cooker, melt snow to heat water, and prepare a full, hot meal for them. The dogs immediately understood the drill, and probably understood that the Boss had a few problems of his own. They ravenously consumed the snacks and immediately curled up on the snow in the formation of the team, diligently cleaning the remaining ice from their fur, and settled in for a nap.

No doubt Cor had known we were coming—he probably heard our "out times" from Dawson on a Whitehorse radio station. I stiffly pushed open the heavy door and was flooded by the warmth of the cabin. I noticed another man, awake, a trapper I had met briefly several years before. He said that he and Cor had agreed to rendezvous at this cabin tonight to watch the Yukon Quest teams come through en route to the finish at Fairbanks. It was a welcome break from their solitary work in the woods, and they knew that the warm sanctuary of the cabin would be hard for the mushers to pass up.

I reintroduced myself and told the man about my incident. Surprised, he told me that the trailbreakers on snowmachines had passed just twelve hours ago and had not reported any overflow. I leaned over the hot woodstove to thaw out the zippers of my suit so I could begin extracting myself from my icy tomb. I looked directly into a giant pot of fresh moose stew filled with home-grown rutabagas and potatoes, which had been kept through the winter in the root cellar. It smelled wonderful.

My zippers started to thaw and drip. I fought my way out of my suit and hung it up by the stove, heavy and sopping wet, wondering if it could dry out enough in six hours so that I might maintain my race schedule of resting and running. It started to dawn on me that I was going to be okay. I put on the dry clothes that I always carry in the sled and went outside to feed the dogs again.

Throughout the time that it took for me to thaw and then redress, Cor remained quietly asleep and did not appear to have moved from his original position beside his open book at the table. I told the trapper that I actually knew Cor fairly well, and that we had raced together several years before. Did I mention that there was also a half a bottle of rum on the table next to his book? I wasn't sure which had put him to sleep—the book or the rum—but I had a pretty good idea of the whereabouts of the other half of that bottle.

I talked to Cor's partner and said, "It's been quite a while since I've seen Cor, and it would be great to talk to him. It's been a couple of years—do you think it would be all right if I woke him up?"

He hesitated, looking very cautious. "I don't think you really want to do that."

"Really? Cor and I have known each other off and on for years," I replied, still convinced that Cor would want me to wake him up. I obviously wasn't reading his buddy's body language very well. The message that he was politely trying to send to me was not getting through.

"He wasn't in that good of a mood when he tipped over," he said. "You ought to leave him alone."

Well, that's a disappointment, I thought. I continued about my business of hanging up my clothes, wringing out socks, and trying to get my gear dry. Though I made every attempt to complete my chores quietly, the crowded cabin was small and the commotion must have been too much. Suddenly, like a Jack-in-the-Box, Cor sat up straight and tall, eyes wide and looking directly forward. With a long blink of his eyes and a shake of his head, like it or not, Cor was waking up. Turning his shaggy head, he blurted out in a loud, theatrical voice, "I killed a moose with a tomahawk!!!" He was a Canadian who spoke English, his second language, with a strong French accent.

I swear, those were his exact words. Admittedly I was taken aback and was totally caught off guard by his announcement.

He repeated in a louder and more emphatic voice, "I killed a moose with a tomahawk!!!" I think he suspected that I didn't believe him.

Good Lord, I thought, *Pandora's Box has opened*. Having darned-near just drowned, I was now hoping that Cor would go back to sleep, and we could start this scene all over again. I had already experienced enough adventure this early morning.

The trapper interjected on Cor's behalf and told me, "He actually did kill a moose yesterday with an ax. A moose was floundering in deep snow, and Cor snowshoed over to it and put it down with his little Hudson's Bay ax." I now appreciated the moose stew simmering on the stove with a different perspective. Cor, in the rough spirit of the woods, was having a little celebration and undoubtedly was a bit intoxicated. He was proud of the incident, but he was also not too sure I believed him. It got a little tense for a while until I calmed my old acquaintance. Soon Cor's head settled back onto the table and, of course, I wasn't going to wake him up again.

Finally warmed, I began thinking and focusing back on the race. I put my competitive game face back on. The dogs were fed and resting, my clothes were drying, and it was time for me to retreat to a back room and a cot. I needed some sleep, at least a catnap, to carry me through the next leg of racing—a six- or eight-hour run to the village of Eagle, Alaska. With a couple hours of sleep and a dry set of long johns, I would be ready to hit the trail again.

When I fell into the open water, my primary concern had been saving me and my dogs. Weighing heavily on mind, too, was the well-being of my competitors who I knew were at least two hours behind. Many of the front-runners were very good friends of mine whom I had traveled with on many occasions in other races. I was sick with the thought that my dogs' tracks might have led them directly into open water.

Under the circumstances, it would have been impossible for me to engineer another route through the overflow. It had been pitch dark and totally indecipherable on the river with a thick fog, not to mention the fact that I was in a critical race to get myself to safe shelter before I froze into a distant memory. I was two hours ahead and it would have been suicidal to wait for the following mushers. My only reasonable plan of action had been to keep going. There were no options. Nevertheless, I was concerned about the fate of my fellow mushers. I hoped that the dim light of morning would help them see my mistake and give them the alert to look for a way around the danger.

Later I talked my friend and fellow racer, Bruce Lee, who was among the following pack. He was able to put the pieces of the puzzle together that morning and had realized that I had followed the marked trail into a deluge of overflow water. Conversely, he wondered about my well-being, after seeing my tracks enter and reappear from a channel of open water. He broke trail with his dogs around the worst overflow, but he still came out the other side soaked and wet to above his knees.

Days later, I wore my new moosehide mittens as I crossed the finish line of the 1989 Yukon Quest first and as the race champion. It was with a huge relief and a certain amount of sheer amazement that I crossed under the finish banner realizing all that had transpired to get me there. Donna and the girls greeted us in the chute, reminding me of the priorities that had helped guide me down the trail.

Joe's Notes

I called Bruce Lee in August of 2007 to test his memory of that cold February night on the Yukon River in 1989. Bruce recalled the chaos as the front pack, in pursuit of Jeff King, entered the overflow zone and saw that King had followed trail markers into a lake of recent overflow—the bane, the nightmare, of a musher traveling in the dark of night.

Of that group, he recalled Kate Pearson, Sonny Lindner, Jerry Riley, and Freddie Jordan. The night was filled with the calls and yells of mushers asking the others if they had found good trail. Headlights blinked and flashed incoherently on the mile-wide bed of the Yukon. Incredibly, all survived, but not without their own adventures to report.

Freddie Jordan, a race rookie from Tanana, Alaska, and my old trapping partner, is an Athabascan Indian, born in a trapping cabin on the Yukon. Still, he was disadvantaged because he did not know the lay of the trail. Jordan was drenched in the same area of overflow, and in a desperate move for survival, he broke trail with his dogs to the far bank of the Yukon. He cut green spruce boughs and made a "bed" on top of the snow—a dry area to change into his spare warm gear. He then scrounged wood and built a fire on the spruce-bough bed, so it wouldn't bury itself in four or five feet of snow. Somewhat recovered, he walked back to the overflow area, got wet again, and rerouted the trail away from the overflow for the following mushers. Freddie received the Sportsmanship Award for the 1989 Yukon Quest for his thoughtful efforts.

CHAPTER NINE

Close Encounters

I have been living on the same property on the East side of Denali National Park for almost thirty years, gradually building our kennel operation, business, and home on a gentle rise facing south onto a little 3-acre body of water we call Goose Lake. A beautiful spot to call home.

Years ago during a dinnertime math project, our daughters calculated that I had traveled more than 150,000 miles behind my tireless Alaskan huskies, and mostly in remote areas of Alaska. Over the years I've wondered if I have taken for granted some of the things I have seen on the trail, particularly wildlife sightings. If you have ever visited Denali National Park, you know that wildlife in this area would rival Marlin Perkins' *Mutual of Omaha's Wild Kingdom*.

For instance, grizzly bears visit our Husky Homestead once or twice every summer. Normally it is an uneventful courtesy call, and they just pass by without giving us a problem. They seem to understand that ninety snarling, barking dogs in one spot are just a little too much to negotiate. In thirty years, I've had to shoot only two problem bears in the yard. These two just refused to leave us alone. But the others, which have included dozens of sightings near my dog yard, made just a brief appearance and then moved on their way.

We've even had wolves come into our yard. From the Homestead picture window, I've watched wolves play on frozen Goose Lake in the winter, romping from one end of the lake to the other. My dog yard is just behind a natural rise not far from the lake, and although the dogs could not see the wolves, they were aware of the intruders at play not more than 100 yards away. In the silence and cold air of winter, sound travels well, and our dogs don't miss a note. I saw one a wolf sit down on the ice and howl—followed by the reply symphony of yodeling, yipes, and howls from the sled dogs. From inside the house, I have observed several wolves following with another rendition of a howl, and creating a battle of the canine bands that would continue for several renditions. Alaska's version of *American Idol.*

Wolves are very prevalent in this area of the state. I don't want to get into the emotional controversy that surrounds wolves, but I will say this: If you have heard of a place in Alaska where some people think wolves should not be managed in any way, and others believe that the wolves are eating "our" moose and caribou and should be managed like other big-game animals—this is the place. Personally I think management compromises have been worked out, and as I write this book, most of the controversy seems to have been negotiated to the satisfaction of many.

From personal experience in traveling hundreds of miles on remote trails training my sled dogs, I can report that this region is chock-full of wolves. Although I rarely see one, I do see countless fresh tracks in the snow that were not there a day before. The wolf is a very cautious and careful animal, and normally they will hear, see, or smell my dog team—and vanish—long before I am able to catch sight of them.

I can't help but be in awe of wolves and what they can do. They are big, powerful animals and much different than the sled dogs. An average adult wolf can weigh anywhere from 85 to 115 pounds. I have talked to trappers who tell me that a giant male may tip the scale at upward of 150 pounds. The power and killing instincts of these extreme predators is awesome to observe.

YEARS AGO, A LIGHT, fresh snow had fallen during the night and completely wiped clean all signs of tracks on the winter landscape. My plan had been to train a team of dogs that morning. The sun was just beginning to shine and started to break through the low-lying clouds left from the snowstorm. A 2-inch skiff of snow gave the landscape that freshly painted look, and the world was clean and new. It was perfect for a person like me, who likes to read the stories of animals left in the snow by their tracks.

I have to confess that I was a little bummed out during that winter because the Alaska Department of Fish and Game, for whatever biological and political reasons, had closed my area for the harvest of caribou. Their logic suggested that the caribou population was down, but some people in my community thought it might have something to do with the wolf politics. It was certainly not my place or area of expertise to make a judgment, so I went along with the decision. However, I was disappointed, even a little distraught, and will freely admit that I enjoy hunting and providing fresh wild meat for my family. I truly missed the opportunity to put caribou on the dinner table that winter. Sure, we could go to Fairbanks and buy some expensive beef steaks from the Lower 48, but I have always found the caribou numbers abundant and looked forward to the annual harvest. It is just one more activity that adds to the richness of my life, as I could be training my dogs on remote trails and simultaneously remain on the alert for a caribou to fill the freezer.

Wolf, 1994 pencil.

This is one of six images included in a Wildlife Portrait Portfolio. As Donna says, "I am enthralled with eyes as 'the mirror to the soul,' so that is the emphasis of this grouping."

On this particular morning, with the sun's rays bright on the fresh snow, I hooked up a ten-dog team for a training session. We left on my trail out of the yard, circled around the house, and headed out into the valley.

Since childhood I have been fascinated, intrigued, and pre-occupied with identifying animal tracks. As a young adult in Sonoma County, California, I was an avid track-reader and enjoyed interpreting whether a print was a raccoon, squirrel, fox, porcupine, coyote, or whatever else I would spot in the mud or wet ground near my home. Reading tracks is something that you just do if you enjoy tromping the woods, and it is particularly interesting in the winter for the woodsman to look for tracks in the snow. It passes the time while you ask questions: "What is it? What is it doing? Where is going?" For me it is a wonderful story left by nature to interpret.

As I departed that morning, all I could see were the tracks of my sled and my dogs. Ahead, the trail was a clean slate. *This is going to be an interesting day*, I thought, because I was going to figure out what all my wild neighbors had been up to this early morning.

About 3 miles from the house, I noticed a track of a single wolf standing out on the clean, white snow like a neon sign. I could tell by looking at the track that he was walking along, but clearly not in a big hurry. I had a pretty good feel for evaluating tracks after watching the different gaits of my dogs for years, and this wolf was just a carefree character walking in the early-morning sun.

I could see where he had walked out of the woods and then turned onto our trail. He was probably finding it easy walking on the packed trail, and we were traveling in the same direction. Taller and bigger than my dogs, this wolf was no doubt swinging his long legs in a lazy, relaxed pace. I calculated we were within thirty minutes of our casual, lone neighbor. It was obvious that my race dogs were traveling at a much faster pace than the wolf's slow amble—probably covering ground twice as fast. I chuckled, not at all worried about a confrontation between my dogs and the wolf. I thought it was quite possible that we might give the big guy a little morning wake-up surprise, zooming up on him from behind.

I was fascinated, and I searched for the moment when his tracks would change from that of a walk into a high-speed lope, the point when the wolf would undoubtedly sense our presence. It was not likely we would actually see the wolf. Their natural instinct is one of caution, and they would prefer to slip into the woods out of sight. Our lone wolf would probably jump off the trail and retreat to some thick cover.

The further we traveled on top of the wolf's tracks, the closer I knew we must be. Point A, the sled dogs, and Point B, the wolf, were quickly converging. Sure enough, about 2 miles after I first saw the wolf's trail emerging from the woods, his tracks changed from a slow walk to that distinctive gait of an all-out explosive run. While trotting, the two sides of the wolf's tracks mirror one another, but the gallop, or all-out run, is asymmetrical and easy to distinguish. Even if you don't understand the mechanics, you can definitely see there is a difference when it is printed out on the fresh snow.

I thought I was pretty smart, quite the expert—just my dogs and me out in the woods—and thought I knew what was going to happen next. But, instead, what I saw next completely baffled me. There, in the middle of the trail, a caribou was lying on its back in the last throes of death. I thought I was seeing things. I started to question my tracking skills. *Was this caribou running on the trail wearing wolf mittens as an early-morning practical joke?*

The dogs had a little different way of interpreting the event, and they were suddenly in an all-out lope themselves to get to the caribou. I stood on the brake and tried to talk the dogs into a "Whoa." Eventually, just short of the caribou, I got them stopped and anchored the team with my snow hook.

Sure enough, I was able to see those loping wolf tracks leading right to the caribou. This was a real-life drama of the hunted and hunter, the prey and the predator, and just seconds old. With the dogs under control—more or less—and the ice hook securing the team, I took a walk to the front for an inspection. The caribou had a hole in the back of its neck—big enough for my fist. The base of its neck was so damaged that it looked like a bazooka had been used. As I stood there the caribou shook for the last time and was done.

Now I could see what actually had happened. Initially I interpreted the tracks to say that the wolf had broken into a lope to avoid my dogs and me. Instead, it appeared he had stumbled on an opportunity to whack a caribou that was not paying attention. The caribou had made a mistake—must have been dozing. The wolf took advantage of the chance encounter and was able to bring it down single-handedly. Although the caribou was not extremely large, it was still much bigger than the wolf. Furthermore, it appeared to have been no contest. There was little evidence of any kind of struggle. The wolf had been quick, decisive, and effective.

Unfortunately for the wolf, we'd come along to ruin his party, and he'd taken the path of discretion and retreated into the safety of the woods. I had a hunch he wasn't too far away. It was an eerie feeling, knowing the wolf could probably see me, although I could not see him, and that the wolf was still seriously contemplating his easy morning hunting trip.

Then I started thinking—the Alaska State Department of Fish and Game said I could not *shoot* a caribou. They didn't have anything in their rulebook about wolf road-kill! I carefully looked that caribou over. There were no injuries or bite marks on the main body that could possibly damage the meat.

Nervously, I pulled my dog team up to the side of the caribou and rolled a winter's worth of meat into my sled. I turned the team around and was back in the yard for one of the shortest one-hour training runs of the year. Donna and I spent the rest of the afternoon butchering the caribou and putting away some excellent meat to be enjoyed the rest of the winter.

On one brilliant spring day, the dogs and I were traveling up the Yanert Fork of the Nenana River and encountered tracks on the trail that indicated a wolf was ambling along at a slow trot. My team of race dogs does not do anything casually. It's just their instinct to travel fast, and with a good trail they will be either trotting at a high speed or shifting gears from time to time to a blistering, ground-covering lope. One of my biggest training challenges has been to teach the dogs to slow down at times.

As we ate up the trail to get within hearing distance of this casual wolf, again I expected to see the tracks change anytime now to an extended lope—but as usual I doubted we would see the wolf. By its collected experience, the wolf surely knew that we came up this broad valley all winter. As I noted before, the wolf prefers a safe strategy of aversion, and I expected he would put it into high gear and disappear into the brush.

Sure enough, within a mile, the gait of our mystery wolf changed into an all-out lope. He must have heard us coming and thought, *Well, here comes that sled-dog guy with a bunch of crazy huskies. I better get scarce.* By his tracks, it was clear as a written message: "Wolf is now running hard to escape advancing sled dogs." Of course, I was not a threat to him, but his natural caution about man was too overwhelming to take a chance on me.

But this story suddenly took a twist. Up ahead, I could see a mysterious steaming, red object. As we advanced on the loping tracks, the object began to appear like prime rib fresh off the butcher's counter. I stopped the team and anchored them with my snow hook for a closer look of what was obviously a fresh

Autumn on the Teklanika, 1989 watercolor.

A lone wolf enjoying the quiet of the new snow on the Teklanika River.

chunk of meat about the size of a Christmas ham. I could see where the wolf had stopped, put his rear and front feet together, arched his back, and heaved-ho with an emergency regurgitation. The wolf realized he was packing excess cargo in his gut, and in order to escape the crazy guy with the wild sled dogs, he made a voluntary, conscious decision to jettison some excess weight.

What a story, I thought. It was important to that wolf to have the capacity to run as fast as possible and lose himself in the subtle terrain of the broad Yanert River valley—fairly open country with miles of low-lying brush and tundra. This wolf put it all together, weighed all the possible consequences, and based on his knowledge, decided to give up a meal and run another day. He'd made a command decision: "These crazy sled dogs are gaining on me, and I have to unload the truck."

Incredibly, the meat did not even look chewed. It was a graphic nature study. Had I not been a firsthand observer, you can bet I would have doubted that a wolf could have ingested that much meat with a single swallow. It looked as big as a loaf of bread.

Now, if you're astute, you will ask if the wolf was possibly trotting along with his share of the kill in his mouth, and that he had never swallowed it. (Good observation, if you did, because I asked that same question.) However, the tracks in the trail contradict this theory. Why would the wolf stop and plant his feet, if all he had to do was loose his grip on the meat? He could have done that at a dead run.

As one would expect, the drama of the wolf occurred within seconds of my appearance, but I never saw the wolf. He expertly jumped off the trail, and despite the wide, open vistas of the valley, he melted into the landscape, undetected.

Canus lupus is a fascinating animal, and I treasure the experiences and encounters I have had with this elegant creature. As a footnote, I should add that I have never had wolves attack my sled dogs. Several times I have seen wolves walking leisurely at the margin of my dog yard, just out of reach of my picketed sled dogs. Although my dogs were in a frenzy of barking and excited by their visiting cousins in the yard, the wolves acted as if they themselves were on a leisurely day trip. One behavior I distinctly remember is the wolves' apparent disinterest and disdain for the chaotic displays of my sled dogs. As far as I could see, they never looked directly at the dogs, but they sauntered by with a look of supreme dominance and confidence. In truth, a wolf physically could make short work of a dog, but they always walked by harmlessly and then evaporated silently back into the wild.

ALTHOUGH MY FIRSTHAND wolf encounters have been rare over the years, I can report that I have seen hundreds, if not tens of thousands, of caribou in my travels with sled dogs. One sighting, however, is as distinct in my memory as an encounter with a wolf.

It was in November of 1992—the night before Thanksgiving. It was already growing dark by late afternoon at the Homestead, and light snow was falling as I readied my third team of the day for their training run.

I was particularly anxious to get this show on the road in the evening darkness, because I had been working diligently over the past few weeks to perfect my headlamp. By mid-winter in this part of Alaska, the sun is just barely skirting the horizon. Days are short and nights are long. By December 21, winter solstice and the shortest day of the year, five dim hours of daylight is about all that we'll see at our latitude in Denali. Since we are often training and racing in the dark, every competitive musher knows that a good headlamp is imperative.

I had been experimenting with boosting the voltage, using gas-filled bulbs, and modifying the reflector of my lamp in an attempt to raise the performance bar and create the brightest light yet on the Iditarod race trail. I was excited about some ideas I had developed and was anxious to put this prototype to the test. Engineering improvements in mushing equipment is almost as much fun for me as mushing itself. Over the years I have spent more and more of my time consumed with "thinking outside the box" to develop better training practices, towline and harness configurations, and equipment innovations. But this particular week, the light of the headlamp was my focus, and I was curious to try out the new combination.

Blasting out of the dog yard, I was relieved to be back on the sled for my final training run of the day. The dogs took off with a swiftness that comes from waiting; waiting all day for their turn to run. Within seconds we were far from the barking dogs left behind and the high-powered yard lights of the kennel.

Fresh snow softened the spruce-lined trail, and the runners slipped silently. It was an especially quiet night. The new snow dampened the sounds of the dogs' heavy breathing and the occasional jingle of the harnesses and tug lines. The stars hid behind the clouds so all I could see were the dogs illuminated by the bright white light of my headlamp.

Our route that night would be the same 15-mile loop I already had run twice earlier in the day. After leaving the yard, we dropped down off the hill from the house onto the Ravine Creek Trail that leads us east toward the Yanert River valley. The river was not yet safe for travel, as it would be another few weeks before freezing temperatures locked up the river with safe ice and provided an additional highway of training trails. I watched through the light of my headlamp as the dogs ran, assessing their abilities as intently as one studies a complex math problem. Their aptitude, desire and talent—it all matters—and I concentrated and watched them carefully. So far, I was impressed with my new light as I continued to test its range and brightness.

Range was an important feature because I often need to locate trail markers in a race. If the wind blew down a couple of markers, a long-range beam on my headlamp could help me spot another marker a quarter of a mile away in the darkness. The trail markers, in most races, have reflective tape on the top of the marker. So, a good headlamp is a big tactical advantage.

All the while, I looked forward to the end of my day. By the third run of the day, dinner is over, it's dark, and I'm tired. This team deserved my attention as much as the ones before, but still I looked forward to spending a few precious moments with my girls when I returned—perhaps reading them a bedtime story. I was eager to relax with a glass of wine and talk to Donna about the day's events. But before that could happen, there was work to be done.

Halfway around the loop, my headlamp's beam caught the glowing reflection of eight pairs of eyes. The shining embers— illuminating like cat's eyes in the dark—were ahead of us and off the trail to the right. I was sure we had come upon caribou bedded down for the night. During the winter months, it's not uncommon to run into these herd animals on the trails around our home. Along the trails, it is easy to read the story of a small group pawing in the snow in search of lichen during the day, and curling up to bed down in the soft snow and tundra at night. It is so common—I hardly reacted to their presence.

I did, however, use the encounter as a training opportunity. Sled dogs love to chase wildlife. As they get excited, I encourage them by whispering, "Moose! Moose!" the verbal cue I use anytime they get worked up. The dogs have learned to associate "moose" with any exciting encounter, and it's just another button I can use if I need a little speed. Just hearing the word, they run harder and faster. It is a cue that I use sparingly so as not to diffuse its value. It has come in mighty handy in the last miles of a close race.

Kobuk Magic, 1989 watercolor.

"Moose! Moose!" I called, and I felt the handlebow lurch forward as the dogs surged ahead. Feeling the power of a dog team is just another added thrill that makes my job description as a musher hard to equal. Every time I feel a team of huskies really lean into the harness at a full lope, my regard for these animals increases.

I rode the brake to keep the dogs from getting too close, too soon, to the small group of caribou. My improved headlamp cut through the darkness as I watched the glowing eyes lift off the ground and the caribou began to mill about nervously.

As the team and I advanced down the trail, the herd exploded

Denali neighbors Bruce Lee and Jeralyn Hath were mushing separate teams in the Kobuk Valley when they were swallowed up by a herd of caribou numbering in the hundreds of thousands. Instinctively, caribou run parallel to their predators until they can get enough distance ahead to change direction safely. Their story inspired Donna's painting.

out of the snow, running directly toward the trail. We were on a crash course if one of us did not alter our direction immediately. The caribou acted as if we were chasing them, but, in my experience, they were not responding as I expected. Usually caribou respond like the classic prey animal and always bolt away from my dog team. I figured they'd run off in the opposite direction—but there they were, heading straight toward the trail ahead of us. I stomped on the sled brake and managed to stop the team to avoid a collision.

The powerful beam from my new and improved headlamp singled out one animal, a massive bull with antlers the size of an entire high-backed dining room chair. In among the younger bulls and cows, he stood out as the herd charged straight across the trail just inches in front of my lead dogs. I zeroed in on the magnificent creature with my brilliant, white light. It is unusual to see a bull with such a huge rack that time of year. The larger the antler, the earlier in the winter they are shed. Generally speaking, a big bull like the one in the beam of my headlamp will drop his antlers sometime in late October. Maybe, I thought, this bull had stayed in the fall rut two or three weeks longer than normal.

I didn't expect any trouble from the bull. Interestingly, caribou bulls do not actually defend their herd of cows. A big bull will define a territory and fight off his competitors and let the cows come to him. The cows, unlike the bulls, actually keep their little racks through the spring and birthing season.

The rest of the herd continued across the trail and disappeared into the darkness, but the bull changed its course. It was as if the headlamp were a lasso tied around its neck. The bull followed the lamp's beam in a sweeping arc around the team and then headed back to the trail behind us. I didn't realize at this point that the light from my lamp was having such a magnetic effect on the bull caribou.

I stood firmly on the brake to keep the team stopped and watched the big bull. As I drew him around in a circle, he followed the light like a beacon. I made a full turn on the sled runners as I followed his path along side and then behind us. I ended up looking in the direction from which we had just come. I trained my lamp on him carefully. Only in retrospect did I realize that he clearly was aggravated.

The bull caribou left the deep powdery snow and charged on to the firmly packed trail behind us. As his hooves met the hard surface of the trail, he pivoted sharply, not as I would have guessed, away from us, but right in my direction. His demeanor changed completely as he gained solid footing. Like an old silent movie, the scene unfolded.

There were no sounds in the dark—only a flurry as the maddened animal charged in blind rage. His head and antlers went down low. His front hooves kicked high and his electric eyes in my headlight beam were fixed on me. He charged relentlessly down the trail in my direction as if I were a matador. Instead of a red cape, this big bull wanted to stomp the threatening brilliance of my light.

Surely he'll turn, I thought. *Caribou don't charge.* In all my encounters with hundreds, if not thousands of caribou, I was confident he would veer off the trail soon. I redirected my light so the animal could see. I mustered up some lung power and let out a war whoop—"Wahhh!"—to end this thing that I had inadvertently begun.

But it was too late. The caribou did not slow its charge and I realized that this big bull was in an instinctive frenzy and was too close to stop even if he wanted to. A caribou bull usually weighs 350 to 400 pounds, but a big bull like this one could weigh up to 700 pounds. I frantically twisted away, covered my head, and braced myself.

One antler met with the seat of my pants. The other clocked me in the head. The animal's skull crashed into my forearm. I was airborne. I instinctively tightened my grip on the sled. The weight of the sled was my lifesaving anchor to the earth. The first rule of a serious dog musher is "Don't let go." It served me well this night.

I found myself facedown in the deep powder by the side of the trail, still hanging onto the tipped-over sled. Caribou are experts at accurately striking with their front hooves in self-defense. I waited for the reign of blows that were sure to follow.

As it happened, on impact with the ground, I had landed on

the push-button switch of my headlamp and turned it off in the fray. Now the world was pitch black.

I curled into a ball as I kept a panicked grip on my sled. Losing my team now would snuff out any hope of escape. I listened for movement above me. My eyes peered out into the darkness. I imagined the big bull looming over me, ready to strike like Mohammed Ali, glistening with rage, towering over his fallen adversary. My heart pounded, my forearm ached, and my shoulder cried out in pain, but the rest of my body seemed in working order.

Still curled to protect myself, I pulled up to the handlebow, righted the sled and screamed at the dogs to go. Not daring to look up for fear of getting an antler in the face, I stayed crouched down behind the sled bag as the dogs leaned into their harness. Within seconds they pulled the sled back onto the trail and we were off at a lope. I relaxed my grip and peered up from the handlebow into the night. I finally worked up the nerve to try my headlamp again and aimed the white beam of light behind me.

Nothing. Not a single caribou in sight. The big bull had slipped into the black sanctuary of the night.

I carefully inventoried my working parts as I cruised down the trail and replayed the events in my mind. With my good arm firmly attached to the handlebow, I used my aching limb to rub the lump on my head and the bruise on my behind to confirm that the encounter with a bull caribou was not just a nightmare. I groaned and moaned, but my dogs were unsympathetic and more interested in blasting dutifully down the trail on the return loop to our kennel. With several miles to go, my head cleared and we arrived home after what was, to them, just another training run. I tucked the dogs in for the night and gimped into the house.

The next day, during Thanksgiving dinner, I described the incident to my awestruck family and friends. As they inspected the stubborn lumps on my head and hip, they commented on the wisdom of waking the sleeping monarch. I realized that this was a year to be especially thankful. It didn't take a lot of imagination to realize I was just lucky to be alive to carve the turkey.

And, as for my new and improved headlamp—I guess it was plenty bright enough.

JOE'S NOTES

After reading Jeff's firsthand accounts of wolves, you may be thinking, "Surely wolves, or wolf crosses, would be excellent sled dogs?"

Surprisingly, when I surveyed a group of today's mushers, none could recount any stories, experiences, or memories of wolf-dog crosses used as modern sled dogs. However, in an incredible biography by Jim Rearden titled *Alaska's Wolf Man: The 1915 to 1955 Wilderness Adventures of Frank Glaser*, he authoritatively describes Glaser's life using sled-dog crosses between a Malemute female and a captured wild wolf. Glaser maintained a team of seven to twelve of these crosses and trapped and traveled in areas now encompassed by Denali National Park. Glaser described his adults as weighing 120 to 150 pounds—giants compared to the fast-traveling, modern 50-pound Alaskan husky. Glaser also noted that the hybrid wolf sled dogs required careful handling and firm, but controlled, discipline. The crosses were by nature suspicious and unsure of man, he acknowledged, and the half-wolves, handled improperly, could be dangerous.

CHAPTER TEN

Halfway Jinx

The Iditarod is Alaska's biggest annual event—it's a huge event, and it is still growing. As I write, it's July 2007, and we are preparing for Iditarod XXXVI! I just returned from Wasilla, where I signed up for my nineteenth time. There was a time when thirty-five teams entered in the race was considered "big." This year a record-breaking seventy-one mushers were there on the opening day of sign-ups, with more than a hundred expected to race the next Iditarod—scheduled to start on the first Saturday of March 2008.

This canine marathon started in 1973, and since then more people have summited Mount Everest than have finished the Iditarod Trail Sled Dog Race. Yet, both spectator involvement and musher participation in the race has increased with each year, and all indications are that it will continue to grow.

Imagine what it was like for me to win this race for the first time in 1993. My first Iditarod had been in 1981, and for the next twelve years I was racing sled dogs, for sure, but the big nugget I was after was winning the Iditarod. At the time, the competition favorites were the famous four-time champion Susan Butcher, and Rick Swenson, a five-time champion. The media didn't notice Jeff King, but each day I woke up thinking about what it would take for me to join the short list of champions—to win the Iditarod.

It was a magical run for me in 1993. From the moment we left Anchorage, I felt I was driving a Dream Team. As we neared the half-way point, my team and I had moved to the front and was vying for control to lead the race. With my fearless leaders, Kitty and Herbie, setting the pace, my mind was working overtime analyzing the team and making sure my decisions were sound—it looked like I had a shot at winning this race.

I also had to consider the long-standing superstition in the Iditarod—"the Halfway Jinx." It was said that anyone who'd ever reached the halfway point first—had never gone on to win the race. The media guys liked this story, and if you were around a TV microphone, some reporter usually asked, "Are you afraid of the Halfway Jinx?"

In pure numbers, twenty mushers had reached the halfway point in first place since 1973, and only one of them (Dean Osmar in 1984) had ever crossed the finish line in Nome still in first place. Neverthe-less, a big award waits for the musher who makes it to the halfway point first. GCI, one of Alaska's Premier Communications Compa-nies, is a proud sponsor of the race and provides the "First to the Halfway Point" award each year. This particular year, the prize was three thousand dollars in specially minted silver ingots to the first team into the Iditarod checkpoint.

The name "Iditarod" is a specific place—the location of the old gold boomtown established about 1910. The actual gold strike happened on Christmas Day 1908, by John Beaton and Bill Dikeman on Otter Creek—a tributary of the Iditarod River in the region in southwestern Alaska known as "Iditarod." A small boomtown city sprang up and stayed active as a mining center

Ground Storm, 1997 watercolor.

A Yukon Quest Commemorative print. A team gets caught in a ground storm—blizzard-like conditions that swirl wind and snow only 20 to 30 feet above the ground.

until about 1930. Now all that remain are the broken-down buildings of the general store, the Miners and Merchants Bank, a house of "ill repute," bars, and cafes. Sometimes people use the name "Iditarod" in reference to the entire Iditarod region, but for our story, think of Iditarod as the old ghost town—the recognized halfway point of the Iditarod Trail Sled Dog Race.

I was having a magical run, as was DeeDee Jonrowe, whose team was running like the wind and was in front of me. A perennial contender and a tough competitor, DeeDee led the way as we approached the famous namesake checkpoint of Iditarod. I was not *trying* to be in second place, but since I was, the superstition thing surfaced in the back of mind. I was thinking, *Well, it looks like I won't be first to Iditarod, which solves worrying about the jinx. Maybe by not being first, I can pull off winning the whole enchilada.*

Cruising along in second place, just a short 3 or 4 miles from the Iditarod checkpoint, I found DeeDee Jonrowe pulled over on the side of the trail, just kind of twiddling her thumbs, giving her dogs a snack. She smiled and waved me by, shrugging her shoulders as if to say, "Why don't you go ahead for a while?" Yeah, right, she's not superstitious. Never known for being anything but competitive, DeeDee sacrificed her lead to avoid worrying about the jinx.

What the heck, I thought, *I haven't ever been first to the halfway checkpoint, and I haven't ever won the Iditarod either. A bird in the hand is worth two in the bush. I'm going for it!* So I kept on mushing and idled into the old ghost town for the halfway prize. After a small congratulatory ceremony, I spent the first of my silver ingots at a hot-dog stand right there in the checkpoint. These entrepreneurs had certainly paid extra attention to the business mantra, "Location, location, location." And poking fun at the extremist animal-rights community, their sign jokingly encouraged sales. It read, "You drop 'em. We chop 'em." The all-beef wienie they served, smothered with onions, hit the spot after days on the trail, and it was a pleasant diversion from my intense race focus. I was delighted with the performance of the dogs and felt really good about my overall position in the race. I've always liked the strategy of looking back over your shoulder at the competition.

Despite the dreaded jinx, I am happy to report that the team and I went on to win the race. A magical ride—it seemed we could do no wrong—in which the team performed incredibly, and I had the honor of breaking the so-called jinx.

DeeDee, incidentally, came in second place, just thirty minutes behind us. And, I've decided, worrying about the jinx *is* the jinx

Joe's Notes

Iditarod—the old mining boomtown—serves as a checkpoint on the Southern Route of the Iditarod and lies about 550 miles from the finish in Nome, Alaska. Mushers as well as the media design their strategy around their orchestrated arrival in Iditarod. An early arrival may indicate an overestimation of team strength—the actual cause of the jinx. The idea is to arrive in Iditarod with a team that's well-rested and prepared with strength and reserves for the last half of the race.

In addition, taking the lead in Iditarod, as Jeff did, requires a steely confidence, because the front team is laying down the scent track for the following teams. It is always easier to catch a team to the front than to lead the pack on new trail.

CHAPTER ELEVEN

Your Neighbor with a Jet

I'd just won my first Iditarod in 1993 when I got a call from Alaska Airlines, a major sponsor and long-time supporter of the race. They asked if I wanted to star in one of their TV commercials. I had never been on TV, and I thought, *This is way too cool to pass up.* I made a commitment to their ad production company and soon learned about the proposed project.

The theme of the commercial was based on the slogan, "Your Neighbor with a Jet." Whether you lived in Anchorage or out in the Bush, if you needed something, you could count on Alaska Airlines—"Your Neighbor with a Jet"—to deliver.

Once I committed to working in the commercial, I learned that the commercial actually had several different segments. One of them was a scene where a Native woman was sitting in front of her little cabin, obviously pretty remote, and she says something like, "I am in desperate need of eggs." Well, in the next scene, up pulls a big Alaska Airlines jet, which eases alongside the cabin. If you're tracking the concept, you know in the next scene that the pilot, with a big Howdy-Doody milkman smile, is reaching out of the cockpit window with a carton of eggs. He just happens to be "Your Neighbor with a Jet."

In another spot, a commercial fisherman has just broken a part on his boat, and he is really in a jam because the fishing season is just getting ready to open. "Opening day is tomorrow, and what am I going to do? I need a new propeller!" laments the hardworking fisherman. Don't worry, here comes "Your Neighbor with a Jet." The Alaska Airlines jet eases up to the boat, and an arm comes out of the cockpit with a brand new propeller.

Now, the theme for my segment (and my first starring TV role) was going to go something like this: "Jeff King, Iditarod Champion, drove his team of dogs one step at a time from Anchorage to Nome, but how is he going to get his dogs back home? Don't worry. Jeff has a Neighbor with a Jet." Over the next month, I was going to find out exactly how this plot line was going to be played out.

Initially, the plan was to fly me and my dog team to Seattle, where their production crew had scheduled the shooting on a side runway at Sea-Tac International Airport. Of course, the reason for this extraordinary effort to fly my dogs to Seattle was authenticity. This commercial was going to be the real deal, and they needed a jet handy on the airport tarmac to put in the same frame with my dog team and me. Needless to say, I was excited as heck about being involved in a major TV production.

A couple of weeks before the scheduled shoot date, the Alaska Airlines people put me in touch with their TV commercial production agency, which was an independent media firm. A couple of days later I was put in contact with the production manager, who was a woman who introduced herself on the phone as "Bunny."

Okay, I don't mean to assume stereotypes, but it *did* seem very Hollywood. I mean, her name was Bunny, no doubt about it, and she was very nice and all. It just seemed to fit perfectly—we're in a TV production! Bunny asked me to send some photos of my championship Iditarod sled-dog team, plus any information I could about the dogs.

"We need to be ready here," said Bunny very efficiently, "and I have to know what I am dealing with, so just send me some good pictures of the dogs. Oh, and some of you, too."

As requested, I sent the color pictures of the dogs and me. As you know, the standard Alaskan husky is . . . well, there is no standard. Some of the dogs were flop-eared, some had sharp ears, some were one color, and some of the others were multi-colored. These were photos of the best long-distance sled dogs in the world.

A couple of days later I contacted Bunny and discovered she was very, very, subdued. "Well, Jeff," said Bunny, in a kind of a resigned-teacher-to-student tone, "This is not exactly what we were expecting." I was momentarily speechless. What could I say? I mean, I just sent her photos of the best long-distance sled dogs living on earth. They just won the Iditarod, for crying out loud!

I thought Bunny was just a little disappointed in how the dogs looked photographically. She probably expected more blue eyes and fluffy tails. But it went a little further and got a lot more personal.

"Uh, Jeff, I know you just won the Iditarod," explained Bunny, like my grandmother telling me I had to put on a clean shirt for dinner, "but I'm pretty sure we can dress you up in a way that everyone can be happy with." Whew, *that* made me feel better, at least they could make *me* look like a realistic musher in Hollywood.

However, the bombshell was just getting ready to explode. "But, Jeff," explained Bunny, "the rest of this is just not going to work. We have to find some other dogs, because these dogs just don't look like sled dogs."

"Are you kidding me, Bunny? These dogs just won the Iditarod," I said without thinking.

Bunny kind of backpedaled. "Jeff, we *know* they're great sled dogs—but they just don't look like what the viewer is expecting." There was a big pause. Bunny seemed pretty self-confident.

"Let's not reinvent the wheel here. You just let me take care of the dogs. You fly on down, and we'll get you some gear so you can

Sapphire, from the "gems" litter

Sled Dog Portrait Portfolio, 1994 watercolor.

Martin, from the "magicians" litter

Our puppies are named by themes. They may not have looked like "real" sled dogs, by Hollywood standards, but they were top athletes.

Breshnev, from the "Russian leaders"

Bush, from "presidential candidates" litter. She was in Jeff's Iditarod team in 1991.

look like Sergeant Preston himself." Bunny had a fairly solid idea of where this commercial was going.

Okay, I started thinking, *this really is way easier for me because I don't have to worry about getting the dogs down to Seattle.* Besides, Alaska Airlines, as an added benefit, had given the family a free flight down to Disneyland as a perk. Now I only had to keep my eye on our girls and leave the sled dogs safe at the Homestead. *What the heck*, I thought, *these people are in charge of the commercial, and they ought to know what they're doing.*

Over the next couple of weeks, Bunny sent me some photos of the dogs she had found for us—large, beautiful, overweight Siberians that would be entirely useless as long-distance athletes. They were the Victoria's Secret model dogs—the kind that are fun to look at—but don't bring one home if you want a sled dog. I was really taking a big interest in the entire production, and Bunny was courteous enough to keep me well-informed.

Bunny assured me that she had been in contact with some professional dog trainers—this was the "real world down here in the Lower 48"—and she had everything under control.

"We need a movie-star dog for this commercial, Jeff, because we need a dog to bark." Bunny had located a dog with movie-star credits that was going to stand in as the trusty leader that had taken me to Nome and won the Iditarod. This dog, according to the script, was named Ranger, and he had a very important speaking, er, barking part.

My line in the commercial was supposed to be, "Ranger, would you like to run back home, or would you rather take the Jet?!" Well, Ranger had been trained to bark on command and, of course, that meant he was voting to fly home. Bunny explained that Ranger was professionally trained and had been in all kinds of movies. Bunny had also signed on six Siberians huskies, and they were going to stand in as the team dogs. So it appeared that Bunny had everything under control. I was set with my new movie-star lead dog, Ranger, and a team of Siberians.

I flew down to Seattle a day before the commercial shoot and got a chance to meet Bunny, who was elegantly dressed in a one-piece black, leather suit. Once again, I was revisiting my stereotype of Bunny—and it was starting to get real narrow. However, Bunny soon earned my confidence. She was very nice and well-organized.

Her crew had a make-up trailer on location, right on the tarmac at Sea-Tac, and they made sure that I was "realistically dressed" (at least by Hollywood standards) with fur mitts and an oversized fur ruff. Well, they didn't tell me how to run the Iditarod, and I wasn't going to tell them how to shoot a commercial. I was thoroughly enjoying the experience my first TV production.

After my session in the make-up RV, the six "team dogs" arrived on the set. They were beautiful Siberians, but totally out of control. I am used to handling sixteen dogs at a time, and my standards of behavior were a little different than theirs. Nevertheless, the trainers and stagehands were working hard to make the production happen in a professional way, and Bunny was making every effort to keep things authentic!

Meanwhile, outside Seattle, up some road in the cool heights of Mount Rainier, a couple of Bunny's guys were standing by with truckloads of snow, because Bunny wanted to make everything look as realistic possible. It was late March with mild temperatures in Seattle, so snow was not going to last long, and the guys up Mount Rainier were waiting for their cue to descend. At the appropriate time, they would spread truckloads of snow on the tarmac so that my dog team could stand on some real Alaskan-appearing white stuff. Bunny sure had a lot of details to consider in her search for authenticity.

That morning we had a dry run. I went through the whole make-up drill in the RV and was wearing a huge fur ruff—like nothing I would consider wearing on the Iditarod Trail. We went through the entire script. The Alaska Airlines jet pulled up on the tarmac, and the pilot leaned out of the window and waved.

I wondered how much that cost, to crank up a jet? On cue, I said my line, "Ranger, do you want to run back to Anchorage, or would you like to take the Jet?!" And, right on cue, Ranger barked that he would like to take the jet. Ranger, or the dog that would be Ranger, was a real professional, just as Bunny had indicated, and looked like he had his barking part under complete control.

The dry run was successful, so Bunny had the crew get ready for the big shoot. Bunny was happy about how everything went in the morning. Everybody was located at the proper position, cameras were ready to roll, and it looked like all we had to do was duplicate the morning's drill. Bunny's plan looked brilliant. She even called in a special catering truck onto the tarmac for lunch.

At the same time, word was sent up to the boys in the high country with the truckloads of snow on Mount Rainier to come on down for the big shoot. So while we were having lunch, these guys arrived off the mountain and spread a couple of truckloads of snow on the tarmac so that the set would look like the *real* Alaska.

It appeared that we were ready for the big shoot, and the production schedule was flawless. The dog team of overweight Siberians was brought back in and positioned on the snow, the jet was put on alert, and I was back in my big fur ruff and make-up. With Bunny in command, we were ready to put the commercial in the can.

Ranger, with his movie-star swagger and upright ears, confidently walked up to get in position. But when Ranger got to the edge of the snow, he stopped. Then he began investigating the set, walking around the edge of the snow while his trainer was trying to call him over to position. I could tell Ranger was thinking, *Hey, nobody said anything about actually getting on snow.*

Mr. Hollywood went on strike.

In the background, I could hear Bunny, a little concern in her voice, talking to the trainer, "Come on now, let's get Ranger in position, this snow is melting awfully fast and we've got to get this done."

Still there was no cooperation from Ranger. Clark Gable doesn't like snow.

The trainer, who was really feeling the pressure from Bunny, put a leash on Ranger and kind of dragged him onto the snow. Ranger's masculine, perky, upright Siberian ears started drooping like a hound dog's. He was holding one leg up, then the other, like a little French Poodle going through a mud puddle. Ranger would not put all four feet on that snow. He had this pathetic, sad look on his face, like "What are you doing to me?" Ranger was quickly losing a lot of his star appeal.

This dog, this immaculately groomed, perfect expression of a Siberian husky, it appeared, had never set foot on snow in his life. All heck started to break loose. Bunny was starting to panic as water was spotted running out the sides of the snow pile—and the jet, which was probably standing by at about a million dollars a minute, was still waiting for action. The camera guys looked frustrated, "Come on, let's make this thing happen."

I was doing my part in my big fur ruff and mitts. I had my line down pretty well. On cue, I asked, "Ranger, would you like to run back to Anchorage, or would you rather take the Jet?!"

However, Ranger would not bark. He was having his own existential meltdown standing on the snow. His movie-star masculinity was at serious risk. Although he would now stand in position, he was a shell of his former self. Bunny blurted, "This is a disaster!"

"I don't think Ranger is used to the snow," the trainer apologized. Quite frankly, he looked as pathetic as Ranger.

Well, Bunny was not to be outdone by a movie-star lead dog, and she earned her money that day. She made a quick and creative decision and sent her "key grip" to downtown Seattle to buy a couple of rolls of some artificial white fluff, like the filler for sleeping bags. Then the crew started shoveling out a space in the snow pile meant for Ranger. The extra snow went over to the Siberian stand-in dogs, who didn't seem to mind cold feet. Bunny's crew began spreading a layer of artificial white on Ranger's position like a giant pillow. Bunny's plan was to keep Ranger comfortable and out of the snow.

Remember, Ranger is my authentic Iditarod champion lead dog.

With this done, Ranger approved of the new working conditions. The cameramen hunched over their equipment. I recited my line, "Ranger, do you want to run back to Anchorage, or would you like to take the Jet?!"

Suspense was in the air. A momentary hush suspended time. Then Ranger redeemed himself and barked like a true professional canine movie star. I am sure Bunny was relieved.

The jet pulled up to give Ranger and his crew a ride. We went on to successfully complete the commercial. Ranger added this performance to his resumé, and Bunny put another project in the can. She had performed well under pressure, and her innovative spirit was right up my alley.

While I had a great time working with Bunny on the Alaska Airlines commercial, I was also reminded how great the differences can be between perception and reality. It really makes me wonder.

Joe's Notes

Jeff King's trademark personality trait is innovation—which is probably why he was so impressed with the Bunny's inventiveness. Jeff was really hitting his stride when he won the 1993 Iditarod and was learning what it felt like to drive a championship team of sled dogs. He won Iditarod again in 1996, 1998, and 2006, finishing in the top ten in the intervening years. By any account, he has won more races in modern long-distance mushing than any one musher.

Readers may be interested in the Siberian as a sled dog for the Iditarod. While Siberian teams have competed in the race, their stocky build, sometimes aggressive demeanor, and slow traveling speed have prevented them from being competitive. The Alaskan husky, like those Jeff breeds for endurance and physiological efficiency, has proven genetically suited for long-distance racing.

CHAPTER TWELVE

Elim:
A Small Star in the Night

I've got to get to Elim, I've got to get to Elim," I repeated as I stomped my feet on the sled runners and shifted about to keep my toes working.

It was 1994 Iditarod Trail Sled Dog Race, and the temperature had plummeted to -50°F. The dogs raced across the moonlit trail along Moses Point, a thousand miles into the race. I was on my way to a third-place finish after my 1993 victory, but on this cold night, I didn't care how I finished. I just wanted to get to Elim, where I could warm my body and get a few good hours of rest.

Little did I know that in Elim, I would find not only the warmth I was looking for, but a small part of that seaside village's spirit, which I still carry with me to this day.

Despite the bone-chilling cold, it was the kind of night that only comes a few times during the winter. Amid brilliant stars, the aurora borealis played across the black sky like blue-and-white party streamers fluttering in the breeze.

My feet had gotten damp earlier in the race, but in my rush to leave the last checkpoint in Koyuk, I hadn't changed to dry boot liners. I hoped I wouldn't pay for my haste with frostbite, but right now even that worry slipped my mind as I stopped the dogs and watched the northern lights.

The aurora swerved about the sky recklessly with an intimidating power that put even the dogs on edge—they, too, could see and feel it, as the waltzing lights reflected on the snow all around us. It felt like we were riding under the neon lights of Broadway, but there was no one here to enjoy the show except me and the dogs. Although my mind knew better, my body instinctively crouched when the lights dipped, leaving me feeling as if I were ducking a low-flying plane.

We continued this way for several miles. Gradually the lights dimmed and my mind once again became aware of the intense, extreme cold. I repeated my mantra: "I've got to get to Elim; I've got to get to Elim."

I pulled into the sleeping village at about midnight and parked the sled at the town fire hall. After feeding the dogs and bedding them down, I hobbled inside to be met by a powerful wall of hot air blasting out of giant 4-foot furnaces that were designed to keep the fire trucks warm.

There were no mushers there. Doug Swingley and Martin Buser had already left, and the next teams were hours behind. I climbed a stepladder and got right in front of the heater. I unzipped my snowsuit and let the hot, dry air bake me to the core, like a blistering Texas gale. Afterward I slept more soundly than I had in days.

Now warm, dry, and rested, I loaded up the sled and roused the dogs to continue on our way. It was 4:00 A.M., and the town was asleep. A few lights lit the main street as we left down a steep hill that led through the village and out onto the Bering Sea. There, the trail continued onward to White Mountain and ultimately, Nome.

On the way through Elim, a gang of rowdy barking dogs formed a gauntlet as the trail emptied out onto the sea ice. I immediately noticed one of them—a young pup, barking madly, simultaneously wagging his tail. I watched in amusement as the group filed in behind us, and wondered when the young punk would tire and turn back toward home.

As the village lights grew small in the frigid night, only two dogs followed—an older husky and the pup. They chased us as if they had never seen a dog team before. Soon the old dog stopped, having fulfilled his sentry duty. But the little guy, still full of spunk, ran at arm's length behind the sled, barking and still wagging.

I was impressed with the pup's enthusiasm and I looked at him closer as he ran, shining my light on his small body. The think, glossy coat, well-suited for this extreme environment, was silver and flowing. He bounded like a knock-kneed colt, yet still managed to keep up with my trail-weary team.

Obviously he enjoyed running, and although he continued to howl, he wasn't barking in anger, but more like a cheerleader urging us onward. Now, well away from the village, it was time to discourage this pup and send him home. Even though I liked him, I knew we had a daunting climb ahead of us, and this pup may not be fit to make it on his own.

"Go home!" I scolded, mustering as forceful a voice as I could: "Get! Go home!"

The little dog barked all the more, inching ever closer to the sled as if he wanted to pass. The last thing I needed was a wild pup running amok in my team, so I swung my leg out wide, trying to distract him from his attempts to run ahead.

Now miles from town, the pup still followed. I knew I had to do something. I stopped my sled and tried to sound even more serious.

"Go home!" I yelled, and lunged at the pup, chasing him down the trail.

The pup darted from me, but the minute I turned to go back to my sled, I could hear him running up to my heels again as if this were a big game.

Tiny Trotters, 1990 pencil.

  We continued this way, and soon I could tell that my behavior was affecting my race dogs more than it was this little puppy.

  My team hangs on every word I say. Now they were looking at me strangely, wanting to know what the heck was going on. I could see it in their eyes: *Why is Jeff so mad?* they were thinking. *Why is Jeff scolding, and who's this dog that's causing all this ruckus?*

  There was only one thing for me to do. I had to get the puppy under control, and I had to put my team at ease. But it was -50°F outside, and I worried that now the town was too far away for the little puppy to find his way home.

  The trail ahead would only get worse, or more remote and steep as we made our way up the mountain called Little McKinley. The trail climbs way above tree line—difficult even for conditioned Iditarod race dogs.

  I decided to stop scolding the pup and encourage him to come along. Even though it would be a challenge, the trip would

only be a little more than 25 miles. If the puppy could make it to the top of the mountain, I would carry him to the bottom and on into the village at Golovin Bay.

I began to cheer on the puppy. Immediately he eyed me suspiciously. He had enjoyed the game of cat-and-mouse we had been playing, and now I'd changed the rules without warning.

The pup slipped back for a moment, and I thought he might turn around. I encouraged him some more.

"Come on! Come on! You can do it!" I shouted, and he couldn't resist. He picked up his pace, and within seconds was up next to the sled, running along enthusiastically.

As usual, I stood on the runners holding onto the sled with my good hand as I let my bum hand—the hand I almost cut off in a construction accident six years earlier—hang limp beside me. As the pup came up alongside, he grabbed at my mitten, trying to yank it off my hand. Playing a new game of tug-of-war, we ran along in the cold darkness. As stern as I had tried to be only minutes before, now I laughed despite myself at this new little comedian I had begun to call "Elim."

Golovin Bay is just a little outpost in the middle of nowhere—a quiet little village and friendly people—and is one of the few checkpoints where you can't drop a dog. The mushers are only required to sign in and continue on their way. I wondered what the race officials would say when I came into the village with a pup tagging along behind. I hoped they would understand my predicament.

The sun was just beginning to rise as we neared the summit of Little McKinley, and I turned off my headlamp. We were halfway to Golovin Bay, and Elim was beginning to show signs of fatigue. Still, I was proud of this little pup.

I decided now was a good time to snack the dogs, to give them a short break before heading down the mountain. I stopped and reached into the sled bag to get out the cooler that contained their snacks.

As I walked forward to dip a bit of food in front of each dog, there came Elim, attacking the piles of food like he had never eaten before in his life.

"Get out of here!" I yelled. "What're you doing, stealing food from my dogs? Get out of here!"

Elim blatantly disregarded my orders. He continued to throw himself at the food with a renewed energy that even my dogs didn't care to show. They looked at him curiously as he ravaged the food. They looked at me as if to ask, "What are we supposed to do?"

I shooed Elim away, and he darted from my waving arms. He barked excitedly as if this was yet another game we were playing. I finally walked away from the dog team, Elim following close behind, and poured the pup his own heaping scoop so he could eat there, away from my team. Appeased, he lunged at the feast ravenously.

I snacked the rest of the team and watched as they, too,

wolfed down their food. They had worked up a huge appetite after climbing Little McKinley, and I wanted them to be in fine form for our arrival into Golovin Bay.

It didn't take long before the dogs were finished with their snacks and raring to go. It never ceases to amaze me that even after a thousand miles, the dogs still have energy to run off. I walked down the line to pet each dog and went to stash the cooler into the sled. I looked up and there was Elim, perched on the sled bag, comfortable as a house cat, and looking at me with a cocked head as if to say, "Come on, aren't you ready yet?"

I had begun to wonder what I was going to do with him, and with the impending daylight, I knew planes soon would be flying. I questioned what the spectators and pilots in those spotter planes would say if they saw this dog running behind. Surely they would think I had a loose dog—race rules forbid this, and I knew I would have some explaining to do.

"All right, I'll give you a ride," I said to Elim as he wagged his tail triumphantly. "Just sit still now."

First I put the food bucket into the bag, then in went Elim. I zipped the bag around his neck so that only his head stuck out, and the team took off down the trail. At first Elim rebelled, and I said soothingly, "It's okay, Elim, calm down," all the while patting his head and ears.

Before long, Elim settled into his new Shangri-la, letting out an occasional howl when he needed more pets.

I couldn't help but laugh, realizing that I had grown attached to this pup. I was only 5 miles from Golovin Bay now, where I would send the little fellow home. It dawned on me that I wasn't particularly looking forward to that moment, although I knew there was no other option.

"Geez," I wondered aloud, "I wonder if there's any chance you might need a home, little Elim. Do you think you'd like to come home with me?"

Elim stretched his blockhead back toward me and let out a comedic howl that I took for a yes.

As soon as we arrived in Golovin Bay, I told the race checkers I wanted to drop a dog. I got the response I expected.

"This isn't a dog drop, Jeff, you know that," the checker said.

"Well, this dog isn't from my team. He's a pup that followed me all the way from Elim. He belongs to somebody there. It was so cold last night, I didn't want to leave him as he followed me from town."

"Oh, okay, no problem," the volunteer said, then paused and added, "That little dog followed you the whole way?"

"Yeah, can you believe it? And he didn't get tired until Little McKinley, so I brought him down in the bag. Make sure his owners get him back—I don't want him stranded here."

"We'll take care of it."

"And while you're at it," I said, lowering my voice a little and moving closer, "could you see if maybe the dog might need a home? Because if he does, I'd be more than glad to take him—he'd fit in fine with my dogs. They can let me know in Nome if they're interested. Can you make sure they get that message?"

"No problem," the volunteer said with a wide grin on his face.

Much to Elim's dismay, I pulled him from my sled bag, and he was chained to a nearby snowmachine. I could hear his howls of protest echoing through the village as we took off down the trail on our way to White Mountain. I thought of him off and on for the next twenty-four hours and wondered how he was faring, and if he'd made it back to his home.

Even as I crossed the finish line in Nome and was reunited with my wife and kids, a part of me was wondering about Elim.

There, a race pilot greeted me with a message from Elim's owners, an Eskimo boy named Christopher and his mother. The two had plans to move from the village, and Christopher's mother was concerned what to do with her son's dog.

The note said I could have the dog, that it solved their dilemma.

They would be happy if he could stay with me. They would meet me in Nome and bring Elim with them.

When Christopher and his mother arrived, we met on the street outside our hotel.

"Hello," I said, taking the boy's hand. "You must be Christopher."

"Yes," came the timid response. Christopher's eyes met mine briefly before quickly looking down at the ground.

"Are you sure, Christopher, are you absolutely sure you want Elim to come live with me? Because if you don't, he needs to stay with you. If you think he needs a home, though, I'll be glad to take him. What do you think?"

Christopher's voice dropped again, and he looked at me.

"Well, I really, really like my dog, but I think we've got to move. Mom thinks it's best," Christopher said. "I want you to have him."

I knew that Christopher was torn. The thought of his little puppy joining an Iditarod Trail Sled Dog Race team surely thrilled him, but he was saddened to let his pup go. I had an idea and knelt down so Christopher would look at me.

"I'll tell you what," I said, "if you ever want Elim back, or if the time comes when you're ready to start your dog team and you want a puppy, you just let me know, because I will be glad to either send Elim back or send you a new puppy."

Christopher's eyes lit up and a faint smile spread across his face. This was a deal he could live with.

"Okay," he said, and we shook on it.

As it turned out, Christopher and his mother never did move and never took a puppy. As for Elim, he spent a couple of years training with us, then moved to a slower recreational team down the road. He often came for visits before he retired into the hills of California.

Christopher hasn't taken me up on it yet, but I keep hoping that some day he will.

Joe's Notes

At -50°F, the air is calm and dead still, a contrast to the weather that usually comes off the Bering Sea and hammers western Alaska's coastal villages with wind. No human moves in the villages, and life in the Arctic slows and waits for the winds to warm the land. It is a philosophical time for an Iditarod musher, too, especially if you have third place secured, and a trail-hardened team, alone on the trail, boring a hole into the arctic night with a steady trot. The only interruptions in this solitary reverie are arrivals at the isolated Eskimo villages of Elim, just 306 residents, and a collection of 142 inhabitants at Golovin. Life is a compressed, but very full experience, at -50°F.

Small events like this one become major stories—complete with the symbolism of the arctic. Elim, the pup that dared to leave the security of the village, became the subject of newspaper articles and later was featured in a children's book.

BALTO

CHAPTER THIRTEEN
The Colonel

I hope that you don't think that the Iditarod Trail Sled Dog Race is just about a bunch of us hotshots in a big hurry to see who can get to Nome first. I'd be doing you a huge disservice if I did not go into detail about one of the many heroes of the Iditarod—one who has never won the race and, in fact, has never even been accused of being in that much of a hurry: Colonel Norman Vaughan.

In total, Norman participated in the race thirteen times and completed his fourth Iditarod in 1990 at age eighty-four. Unbelievably, he continued to participate in the race for four more years—until he was eighty-eight years old. Sure, in 2006, I was recognized as the oldest musher to have won the Iditarod, but in just thirty-six more years, I could be the oldest guy to ever *run* the race.

Born in 1905, Norman worked with sled dogs growing up in Massachusetts. At twenty-three, he accompanied Admiral Richard E. Byrd on his famous 1928–30 Antarctic Expedition by dog team. Forty-five years later, in 1975, this amazing man was running the Iditarod for the first time. Always a gentleman of the old school and an adventurer in the classic sense, Norman Vaughan is one of my all-time heroes.

I first met Norman in 1981, when I was running my first Iditarod and he was running his fourth. I was twenty-three and he was seventy-seven. He had already lived a long and fruitful life, jammed full of tales and adventures—any one of them would be another's dream of a lifetime.

After Norman's last Iditarod, at eighty-eight years old, he made a formal announcement that he would not run the race again the following year. I was crushed. I thought wistfully, *Oh, man, this must be really hard for him; someone who thinks that much about the outdoors and has tried and continued to run the Iditarod at that age—and now he's going to sit on the sidelines.* All of Alaska congratulated him on this gallant entry into what we thought was his retirement. Clearly none of us really knew Norman all that well.

It was shortly after that announcement that he revealed he was planning another trip. This time he was going back to Antarctica. There was a mountain on that continent that he was determined to climb. This particular summit had special meaning: Sixty-five years earlier, the famous Admiral Byrd had named it for him during an expedition to the South Pole. Norman wanted to climb that mountain before he got too old. He had no doubt that he was going to summit the 10,302-foot mountain that had stood isolated and unconquered on a map of Antarctica since Byrd had named it Mount Vaughan in 1929.

With the support of the National Geographic Society and a famous Alaskan mountain-climbing guide, Vern Tejas, just days before his eighty-ninth birthday, Norman stood on top of his namesake mountain, and became the first person to do so. He returned victorious. Again, the whole state was in celebration and in awe of this man who, by any definition, was an Alaskan hero.

Now, I assumed that surely he was going to settle back and gracefully rest on his laurels. *Norman,* I thought, *you just pulled off another amazing accomplishment to add to your incredible resumé of life.* What could possibly be next, except to sedately retire to the quiet life of a time-honored champion?

However, on a stormy, dark, wind-whipped Halloween night in 1996, a knock on the door of my house would signal the beginning of another Norman Vaughan adventure. I remember that my oldest daughter, Cali, was twelve at the time. Tessa was ten and my youngest daughter, Ellen, was just four. The three girls were very bummed, as only little girls can be, because we had just broken the news that there would be no trick-or-treating that night.

On that particular Halloween in 1996, we had a blizzard that rivaled a northerner off the coast of New England. There were snowdrifts on the driveway that prevented us from getting in or out. We delicately announced to the kids that we would have to postpone trick-or-treating a day or two because there was absolutely no way we could leave our house in this storm. Our declaration went over like a lead balloon.

Here in Denali, trick-or-treating is a little different than where I grew up in the Bay Area of California. On Halloween, when I was a kid, my mother would dress me up in a pirate costume, hand me a pillowcase, and tell me, "Okay, son, just be home before it gets dark." (Around here if I said that to my girls, they would have to be home by late September.) We would then comb the neighborhood, being sure to systematically hit every house (except the dentist's) on every street and finally arrive home with our booty—a pillowcase so laden with candy that it bulged, straining the seams. By the time we got home, the thing would have to be dragged along due to the sheer poundage and bulk. The contents were then heaped onto the living room carpet and sorted according to delectability and trade value. Months would go by before the last of that unending mound of candy was swallowed.

In Denali, we have had temperatures drop as low as -30°F

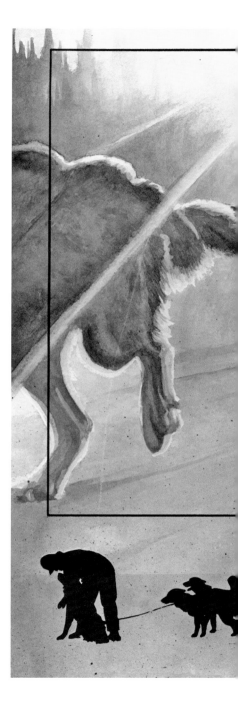

The Freshness, 1989 watercolor.

A Yukon Quest Commemorative print. Titled from Robert Service's "The Spell of the Yukon": "The freshness, the freedom, the farness, O God! how I'm stuck on it all."

on Halloween night. When we'd go trick-or-treating, we'd get the kids dressed in their little Cinderella and Tinkerbell outfits, but that would be just the beginning. Then we'd put on their snow pants, then their parkas, then their hats, mittens, and boots and, before we did anything else, start the truck to warm it up. While the engine warmed, we'd get on the phone with the neighbors to make sure they were home and ready for trick-or-treaters. (We had very few neighbors, and at that time, we also had some of the only children in the neighborhood.) Then we'd trundle along, driving from house to house, visiting six or eight houses in all.

At each stop, the kids would jump out of the car with their tiny, little goodie-bags and race up to the house to knock on the door. Once the holiday chant was made, we'd be invited inside so that the girls could then remove their parkas, snow pants, hats, mittens and boots so as to best show off their costumes. We'd visit for a while, the girls would be awarded with a treat, and the ordeal of dressing all three girls back into their pile of outdoor gear began again. Back into the car and down the road we'd go to repeat the process.

It took most of the night, and the girls carried home a small sack of Halloween treats that meant as much to them as my pillow-case loads ever did to me. Luckily, I had resisted from boasting to the girls about my childhood scores.

Anyway, on this particular Halloween night in 1996, Donna and I postponed trick-or-treating until Mother Nature cooperated. The kids were certainly disappointed, but it wasn't like the other kids would get all the loot—there really were no other kids. Their only competition was our neighbor's little newborn baby.

So we sat down at the dinner table, isolated by an arctic storm. The kids were quiet and melancholy. It was understandable. There was not a lot of conversation going on when, in the middle of dinner, I heard a knock on the door. I immediately thought, *Who the heck is that?* Normally we can see car lights shine in the dining room window if anyone drives up to the house. There were no lights, but the knock on the door sounded again.

Man, I was thinking, *somebody came a long way to go trick-or-treating.* It was seven o'clock at night, in a blizzard, in the dark, on Halloween. *Who could this possibly be?*

I opened the door, and the light from the porch illuminated Norman Vaughan—a big, beautiful smile on his ninety-one-year-old face and snow all over his beard.

"Jeff, I found you," he said in his cultured East Coast accent, adding, "I've been looking for your house for an hour." This was like Michael Jordan showing up at your basketball practice. This is the man who accompanied Admiral Byrd to the bottom of the world, organized rescue missions during World War II with dog teams, and gave the Pope a tutorial on driving sled dogs.

"Norman Vaughan," I said. My kids heard me utter his name. *Norman Vaughan.* They have heard that name all their life, and Norman Vaughan is embedded in their consciousness. All three girls forgot about Halloween. In their little clear voices, I heard them repeat in the background, "Norman Vaughan is here?"

The famous man stuck his head in the door and into the entryway of my house, saw my kids seated at the table eating dinner, and looked to me apologetically, "Jeff, I am interrupting your dinner, aren't I? I'll come back later." And he turned to walk away. Under any circumstance, Norman speaks like a gentleman, and tonight was no different.

I had no idea how Norman had arrived at my house. He was retreating into the blowing snow and had every intention of just fading back into the storm so he would not interrupt my kids' dinner.

I grabbed the big man by the arm, "Come in, Norman. What can I do for you?" I led him into my kitchen. He was a long-time acquaintance of mine, but he had never been to my house. It's true I didn't know he was coming but, of course he would always be welcome. Donna quickly began to prepare another place at the table and I encouraged, "Norman, have some dinner. What are you doing here? How did you get here?"

"Well, I'm on the way back from Fairbanks," said the Colonel, as if he traveled everyday in a swirling blizzard. Fairbanks is 125 miles north of us via the Parks Highway. He had been attending the annual Mushers' Symposium there.

"Alone?" I asked incredulously. I was wondering if *I* would be allowed to drive to the grocery store with an electric golf cart when I reached his age.

"Yes," he continued nonchalantly, "and I finally found your driveway. But I got my truck stuck in a drift at the bottom of that big hill, so I had to walk up the rest of the way." He was ninety-one years old. He had just driven for three difficult hours from Fairbanks. He had gotten stuck in my driveway because he wanted to talk to me. He had walked uphill through a half-mile of drifts in a snowstorm that I would not even take my kids out to go trick-or-treating with a four-wheel-drive vehicle. Then he apologized for interrupting my dinner, and announced that he would "call" again at a more appropriate time.

"Norman, come on in and have a seat for dinner. Spend the night with us. Really, I'll get you unstuck in the morning. I am glad you're safe. Everything will be just fine in the morning. We'll get a bed ready for you after we eat." Of course, I was feeling a bit concerned and responsible. This man had covered a lot of miles. There was no way I was going to let my old friend, famous explorer or not, back out in that blizzard. Besides I wasn't so sure that I wanted to leave my nice, warm house to venture down our driveway in this storm to get his truck unstuck.

"No, no, thank you," said Norman. "I do want to talk to you, but I'm anxious to get home." Home was Trapper Creek—another 120 miles south of us—a drive with a good road. I could imagine that the intensity of the storm was likely to increase as he drove south over Broad Pass and through the Alaska Range.

"Norman, spend the night with us. What's the rush?" I tried to reason with him. He wasn't going to go anywhere on the Parks Highway on a night like this, but I had to exhaust all my powers of reason to convince him.

"Well, Jeff, I have been gone a couple days already, and I'm in a hurry to be home. Carolyn is home alone and I'm anxious to be with her. I didn't really bring in that much wood for her before I left."

"Norman," I tried to come up with some logical reasons to spend the night. He was talking about his wife, Carolyn. "Norman, first of all, if we could even get to your truck tonight, we probably couldn't get it unstuck quickly. Second, when we did get your truck unstuck, I wouldn't let you drive to Trapper Creek in this storm. And, third, Carolyn is thirty-seven years younger than you are and very healthy. I'm quite sure she can bring in an armload of firewood all by herself."

Ten years earlier, Norman and Carolyn had met on the Iditarod Trail, both as Iditarod mushers, making eyes at one another going down the trail—in the singles lane. They had fallen in love and were married. Okay, he was anxious to be home because he missed her, and Norman thought she was going to need help splitting kindling or something—but I had to convince him to stay in one spot until the storm broke.

As the conversation paused, our daughter Tessa sat politely in her spot at the table, uncommonly quiet and concentrated. She's always been very good in math. Unexpectedly, she blurted out, "Dad, that is like you marrying baby Zahn!" She was referring to our neighbor's three-month-old infant. There was a moment of halted conversation before Norman let out a hearty laugh. Donna and I exhaled.

After some concentrated cajoling and some more reasoning, Donna and I finally brought him around to spending the night. I was relieved to know that my responsibility to oversee Norman was satisfied. He would be safe for the night. We sat him down to dinner and finally got around to asking him why he had made this monumental excursion to find me.

"Jeff," he began, "you know, I have been down in Antarctica for the Mount Vaughan climb, and I sold all my sled dogs before I left." By 1988, it was prohibited to bring dogs on the continent of Antarctica. As a result, he had sold all his dogs and traveled by foot.

He continued, "I'm planning on taking a trip, and I'm anxious to put together another dog team, so I'm looking for a couple of good dogs, maybe a leader. Do you have any for sale?"

Norman Vaughan, at age ninety-one, was sitting at my dinner table shopping for dogs. This is the honest-to-God's truth. He was engaged in his role as a crafty dog buyer, trying to talk me out of my best lead dogs, so he could make another trip by dog team.

"Norman, what's next? What haven't you done? What is there left?" I was trying to understand when a man finally decides he's had enough adventure in one life. Everything about Norman Vaughan inspired me.

"Jeff, I want to retrace the serum run." It was a simple statement, but I knew exactly what he meant when he said it. In January 1925, sled dogs were used to carry medicine across the territory of Alaska in a relay race to reach the diphtheria-stricken town of Nome. Had it not been for the courage of twenty mushers—many of them mail carriers and most of them Native Alaskans—and the incredible abilities of their dogs, Nome would have been wiped off the map. The antitoxin had traveled by rail from Anchorage to Nenana, then onward to Nome along 674 miles of winter trails. Handed off from one musher to the next in bitterly cold temperatures, the bundle of antitoxin traveled day and night, arriving in Nome in a matter of days. It made national headlines.

Norman wanted to bring the focus back to the dogs of early Alaska and retrace the exact route that was used in that historic rescue effort. It was also the twenty-fifth anniversary of the Iditarod Trail Sled Dog Race. He thought it would be a fitting way to celebrate the race anniversary while commemorating this heroic run.

Balto was the lead dog of the last team to relay the antitoxin. He got all the fame and glory for that historic, life-saving journey, and he became the symbol of the 1925 Serum Run to Nome. There is a statue of Balto in Central Park in New York City commemorating all of the heroes, both human and canine, who saved so many lives in 1925. Another bronze Balto is displayed on a corner along Anchorage's 4th Avenue, the starting chute for the Iditarod. And at the Iditarod Headquarters building out in Wasilla, Alaska, stands the preserved mount of Togo, another of the heroic sled dogs who were famous nationwide in 1925.

Norman captivated my family that night of the Halloween blizzard, telling amazing tales of his adventures around the world. And true to his word, in 1997, he would go on to organize what he named the Ceremonial Serum Run. Always an organizer and a tireless promoter, he chose the dates to run simultaneously with the Iditarod Trail Sled Dog Race. It just so happened that he also recruited many "recreational" mushers who had originally signed up to run the Iditarod. They withdrew from the race and chose to travel with Norman in an event that had no prepared course, no trail markers, no spectators, and no prize money. But it was grand idea with a high likelihood of adventure and success under Norman's banner.

He even influenced the first woman to ever win the Iditarod, 1985 Champion Libby Riddles, to join his group of mushers. Norman and his group went on to relay a ceremonial package to Nome on the same, exact 674-mile route used by the 1925 mushers. Norman's entourage just happened to arrive in Nome coincidentally on the same day as the Iditarod Race leader arrived at the finish. And, by golly, within only a few short hours of that year's winning team. Well, isn't that astonishing? Now who would have suspected Colonel Norman Vaughan of an intentional promotion?

Jimmy the Greek would pay good money to know what date the Iditarod winner was to arrive in Nome. Norman Vaughn not only figured it out at an advanced age, he also arrived with the ceremonial package carried from Nenana, giving celebration to the 1925 Serum Run and the sled dogs that made it possible.

At the finish line of the Iditarod Trail, waiting for Norman under the burled arch, waited a woman named Edith Iyatunguk, almost as old as he, seated in a wheelchair in a place of honor on Front Street in her hometown of Nome. As a child in 1925, Edith had received some of the diphtheria antitoxin carried by dog team in that historic relay. She was waiting to thank Norman for bringing a focus back to this historic Alaskan event that meant so much to her and the citizens of Nome; one that had saved so many lives, including her own. After quick introductions were made, Norman fondly and ceremoniously handed her the fur bundle of symbolic serum with a brilliant smile on his weathered face.

Norman Vaughan was a grand old adventurer. He and I talked many times, and over the years became very good friends. He came to our house several occasions, including that unforgettable Halloween night, and often with Carolyn. He sat in the audience of my evening program during my Husky Homestead Tours. I put the Vaughans in chairs in a place of honor at the front of the audience. At the end of these programs he would sign his books for visitors.

In 1992, Norman wrote a book titled *With Byrd at the Bottom of the World: The South Pole Expedition of 1928–30*, followed two years later by an autobiography, *My Life of Adventure*. In fact, the day Norman visited my house on Halloween, he had been in Fairbanks signing books. For the past several years, it seemed like everywhere I went for some engagement or presentation, there was Norman signing his books. He would be at a card table at

Borders, or at the local grocery store, or at a musher symposium laughing and talking with his fans as he inscribed each book with his inspiring mantra, "Dream Big and Dare to Fail!" Once I was at the state fair in Fairbanks after having won the Iditarod, signing autographs and promoting the race for the Iditarod Trail Committee. Again, predictably, there was my hero, my old friend, signing his books.

Truthfully, I kept thinking, *Norman, you're getting up there—isn't there something else you would rather be doing than signing books for all of those people who keep asking you the same question over and over?* I knew firsthand some of the challenges of giving presentations for a living, and he had been doing it for twice as long.

"Norman, wouldn't you rather be fishing or . . . something?" I finally asked.

"No," Norman said without hesitation, "I am going to sign my books here today, and tomorrow I'll sign them again."

We had innumerable conversations at these gatherings. I would always approach Norman, at some point, and question his work schedule. I was trying to get through to him, or so I thought, and wondered if he was thinking straight. I continued to ponder his dedication to his rather energetic agenda, which involved hours of disciplined effort selling his books and the grueling marathon of politely greeting his numerous fans.

"Norman, isn't there something you would rather be doing than signing autographs on your books?" I was serious. My question deserved an answer.

He finally looked at me, quite frustrated, with his hands on his hips, and said, "Jeff, I didn't budget to grow this old."

He was, however, determined to make his hundredth birthday. This was a subject he would openly talk about with me during the last five years of his life. Three months before his hundredth birthday, he called and announced, "Jeff, it looks like I am going make it."

"I know; we all know it," I told him. "We are so happy, where's the party? I want to be there."

He said in that even voice of an East Coast gentleman that I had grown to know so well, "Jeff, I want to go to the North Pole for my hundredth birthday."

I knew better than to think he was joking. He was most certainly very serious. He and his wife had made arrangements with the National Geographic Society and had developed a plan to hopscotch him up to the North Pole via some very sophisticated aircraft. He wanted me to accompany them with a dog team and prepare to transport him for the final miles to the Pole.

"Norman," I told him with all the respect and admiration that he deserved, "I would be honored to do that." And we started preparations. But about two months before Norman's big birthday, his health started to fail to a point that prompted his doctors to issue a firm order: "Norman, it's a bad idea. We don't want you to leave the hospital."

He was placed in the hospital in Anchorage, his pacemaker was checked on a regular basis, and although he was as clear-thinking as ever, it was obvious that his body was giving out. Nevertheless, as his wife Carolyn Muegge-Vaughan has since pointed out to me, she and Norman were fully preparing to go to the North Pole upon his imminent discharge. The solution to Norman's doctor's orders were simple: "We're just going to bring Norman's doctor along with us."

I can gladly report that Norman did make it to his hundredth birthday. Although he desperately wanted one last adventure, his physicians kept him under supervision. So there was a huge celebration at the hospital in Anchorage. His whole floor was jam-packed with us fans and friends from around the state. That night he announced to the group that he would have a glass of champagne—and that it would be the first alcohol that had touched his lips in his entire life. Norman had told his mother, in his youth, that he would have a glass of champagne on his hundredth birthday, and she conceded, "That's all right, Norman." He did partake of the champagne with one sip, but said that it tasted awful and did not finish his glass.

He died peacefully four days after the birthday celebration. One hundred years of adventure behind him. Colonel Norman Vaughan was a very good friend to me and an inspiration to us all.

Joe's Notes

Was it chance or coincidental design that Colonel Norman Vaughan arrived in a driving blizzard, in the dark, at the home of Jeff King on Halloween night?

Norman could have purchased sled dogs at any one of hundreds of kennels. But I believe the elderly man chose to challenge his friend. Knocking at the door, covered with snow, the Colonel was putting the test to a fellow adventurer as if to say, "Hey, look what I am doing, Jeff!" I think the old adventurer was having fun with a fellow trailmate on a dark and stormy night.

Jeff must have passed the test. When the time came for Norman's last wish to go to the North Pole on his hundredth birthday, he called on his friend Jeff King to put him in the sled, old and frail, and take him on his last sled-dog adventure.

Chowhound

What makes an exceptional sled dog? How I make the final decision to select a dog for my team is sometimes difficult to quantify. But I do have a shortlist of attributes that we use here at our kennel to help us narrow the selection and identify a really significant sled dog. We'll look for a natural athleticism, intelligence, the instinctive desire to move down the trail, iron-tough feet, quick recuperation time, and the ability to both travel and work continuously over a thousand miles on rough and varied terrain without injury. All are all extremely important attributes. Additionally, we are very careful to try and perpetuate our line of dogs that possess remarkable fur. Their coats must withstand the uniquely diverse Alaskan weather and allow them to stay comfortable in a sometimes brutally cold, as well as not overheat in an occasionally warm (by our standards, that means *above* zero!) environment.

Every one of these characteristics are important, but if I had to line them all up and rank them, at the top of my shortlist would have to be one trait that I haven't mentioned: a strong, consistent appetite.

A number of interesting studies have been undertaken during the Iditarod race to determine how many calories sled dogs will consume to maintain appropriate energy levels without either degrading muscle tissue or tapping into their fat stores. As a point of reference, a recreational sled dog with a very light workload will need roughly 1,500 to 2,000 calories per day during the winter to maintain their condition. My championship race dogs, however, will burn in the neighborhood of 8,000 to 10,000-plus calories per day running out on the Iditarod Trail. This is *five times* the calories needed for a "maintenance" diet, and that is where my dogs go off the charts.

Incidentally, sled dogs must also have *very* efficient metabolisms. I have handled Alaskan huskies every day for thirty years, and I am still amazed at their ability to consume and utilize food for energy, as they run more than a hundred miles a day, for days on end.

How aggressively will they eat? Will they eat when they're tired? Are they particular or prodigious eaters? These are some of the questions that I ask when considering a dog for the starting line-up of my Iditarod team. We actually grade each dog on its appetite—it is that critical. I have learned over the years that sheer athletic ability—which can be impressive during training and shorter races—is always trumped on long-distance races by the more important trait of managing and maintaining their energy balance.

Some of my handlers are puzzled by my choices for our "starting team." They will remember one dog as a fast, hard-pulling, vigorous "jock," and another one as a less athletic performer. But if my more mediocre performer is always packing down the groceries every time I offer some sustenance, I'll guarantee that dog will be the greater superstar by day five on the Iditarod trail. I will *always* select the one that I know will be interested in eating *throughout the race.* And the only way I can really determine this characteristic is by actually testing them, either in hard training and/or during long races.

That is one reason why I think it is so important to have all my promising young dogs run the Iditarod in a "junior varsity" team with one of our handlers. The pace is certainly not at a championship level, but after 1,100 miles over the course of eleven or twelve days, my handler will be able to tell me which of the dogs were always looking to "put on the feed bag."

After a long physical effort on the trail, I always ask, "Did they want to sleep before they ate?" Some of us humans are like that—we just don't want to eat when we're tired. However, when I'm racing I have my team of sixteen huskies on a very demanding schedule—and this simply will not work for a Jeff King Iditarod dog. Upon arriving at a rest stop, they must eat immediately to maintain that all-important energy balance—then sleep. If I have a sled dog that wants to sleep first, and then eat—well, no matter how good an athlete he might be—he is not going to make the cut for my Iditarod team.

Over the years, after watching pups, adolescents, and adults alike (and observing their eating habits), I have had one exceptional—and comical—dog that not only got straight A's in appetite, but received all the eating bonus points as well.

Ever since she was a freshly weaned puppy, sweet adorable little Peg has been a complete "Jabba the Hutt" on steroids in every phase of feasting. She has an appetite that is hard to describe in words, but let me say this: If you were to ever look up the opposite of "anorexia nervosa," you would most likely see a picture of Peg. Through her life she has always been way ahead of the energy curve, and without my intervention, Peg would have been a constant candidate for the "Jenny Craig for Canines" dieting program. The only time her diet is not restricted is on the Iditarod Trail, where she is free to eat all she wants to stay ahead of the incredible energy demands of the race. In this race setting, Peg is the consummate Queen of Cuisine—a truly exceptional animal.

Even as a puppy, she has eaten as fast and as voraciously as she could. In the pen with other pups, she would growl in an effort to keep her position at the feed pan. At an early age, she was already

A Brilliant Future, 1992 watercolor.

Puppies bring with them optimism for the future. These pups dream of being sled dogs.

developing behaviors that guaranteed her more than a fair share of the food, and as she grew up, I found I had to separate her from the rest of the puppies because she succeeded in making her littermates a little nervous. She was all bluff and would never cause a scuffle, but she was an obvious disruption at mealtime. Peg around the feed bowl was always an amazing thing to experience—while most dogs gulp their food, Peg was way beyond that. She sounded like one of those coin-operated vacuum cleaners at the car wash. In retrospect, I should have named her Hoover.

As she grew up, Peg became one of our best sled dogs. In the other performance categories she was getting B's and B+'s, but in the all-important category of appetite, she was setting the curve from the moment she began nursing.

In due time, Peg became an important member of my Iditarod team. In 1999, as part of our pre-Iditarod racing season, I ended up taking Peg (and the rest of our team) down to a race in Wyoming called the International Rocky Mountain Stage Stop Race. In this event, unlike the Iditarod, you race each day from one community to another, covering about 50 to 75 miles each day. Much like the Tour de France bicycle race, you have an opportunity to win each day's "stage," while ultimately competing for the overall race winner—as determined by the cumulative times earned in each stage. The actual race course depended on weather conditions, but the organizers advertised that we would be racing ten "stages" between communities.

The Stage Stop is normally scheduled from the end of January into early February, and therefore it fit into my Iditarod preparations perfectly. With a month until the start of Iditarod (always on the first Saturday of March), this race was a perfect tune-up for my Iditarod team.

On day one, the race starts in Jackson Hole and ends up in the town of Lander. At Lander, the clock stops. You go to a hotel, or a local host family (which is very civilized and my preference), dry out your gear, and get rested up. Also, each community throws a big party for the mushers, families, race volunteers, and visitors on the night they arrive. Then you get a good night's sleep before the next day's race.

I should also add that my dogs were staying in their own equivalent of a Motel 6 on wheels. I have a 26-foot trailer that has deluxe compartments for the dogs, including fluffy straw beds, and places for me to store my equipment, food, gear, etc. As a practical matter, it was also easier for me to keep weight on the dogs, since they were resting warmly in their cubbies and didn't have to burn as much energy to maintain their body temperatures.

On day two, we started our leg from Lander and raced over to Green River. The time was recorded for that day, and the race routine started all over again.

As you can imagine, after spending a few days on the road with the dogs, we develop a routine with our Motel 6 operations. And this drill becomes predictable for both the team and us. The dogs race hard during the day and usually finish late in the afternoon. Once past the finish line, we offer them a snack and some broth and let them cool down. After we remove their booties and unclip their harnesses from the sled, we give them some dinner and then let them rest on fresh straw we have spread out by their "motel." We put them all in their boxes by about 5:00 or 6:00 P.M. While we go to dinner and socialize, we let them sleep until about 11:00 P.M. Then once again we take them out of their boxes to stretch and relieve themselves once more before resting the last part of the night. Early the next morning, they get up and out for another day of racing.

It doesn't take long before the dogs are totally adapted to this life on the road, and I have no doubt that we could simply let all sixteen dogs loose and go through the ritual of feeding and watering without an incident. However, we often find ourselves in populated areas, so it's safer to picket the dogs around the truck, er, motel.

They're clipped with a short lead (about 2 feet long) to eyebolts attached on the outside of the trailer, so that they don't run all over the neighborhood in the middle of the night. This keeps them separated and makes feeding, watering, and cleanup manageable. Since I know where everyone is picketed, I can also keep track of any yappers and make sure that they stay quiet. I sure don't want to wear out my welcome—especially after only a couple of hours in the neighborhood!

I also like to give them a little treat at this point in the night, because again, I'm always thinking about how to supply more calories to the team. One of my "innovation" projects was to develop a very palatable lamb sausage with a known, pre-measured ratio of fat and protein. These sausages come frozen in a 16-inch stick, and since the sausages are a consistent size, it does not take me long to calculate the caloric needs of each of my racing dogs. While some of the big males might need a sausage and a half, some of the smaller, easy-keeping females might require only half of a sausage. If I think one of my huskies needs to gain a little more weight, then I'll bump up his or her treat. My goal is to keep the team in good racing condition—I definitely want them to replace all the calories they burned through during the race, but I don't want them to run too heavy either.

It was in Pinedale, on the fourth day, when—as I had done so many times on this road trip—I reached into the back of my trailer to grab my bag of custom-made sausages for their little midnight snack. Visualize, if you can, that it's pitch dark, we are in another new community, where we have no idea what the neighborhood looks like, and I'm trying to be a good mushing citizen and making every effort to be quiet. The dogs are picketed around the truck so they can relieve themselves before bed. In total darkness, in the back of the trailer by the door, I grabbed my sack of lamb sausages—which I discovered later was inadvertently sitting on a stack of emergency highway flares.

Happy Feet, 1989 watercolor.

Rosemarie takes a moment for a pedicure.

Now, when I pulled out the sack from the back of the trailer, without realizing it, I also dragged some of the highway flares with them out onto the ground. So I'm walking around the trailer giving everybody their lamb-sausage snack, feeling good about things, and I soon returned to the back of the trailer (where I had Peg picketed) to put away my bag.

The beam of my headlamp, however, revealed a disturbing development. In the periphery of the darkness and light, I could barely make out Peg frantically choking down what I thought was an entire sausage. *That's my girl*, I thought. She was certainly displaying another one of her characteristically rude table manners, as between her giant, gagging mouthfuls, she would quickly glance up at me to gauge my progress in her direction. She was determined to get this thing down before I got the chance to take it away from her. But as I got closer, I could see that it was not a sausage at all—it was one of those darned highway flares that had escaped out of the backend of my trailer! She was eating the 16-inch highway flare like it was one of my painstakingly prepared, hand-stuffed, delectable lamb sausages.

Well, it was logical from Peg's perspective—although she would never be compared to having the discerning taste buds of a Julia Child. After all, it was the same shape. "My God, don't eat that, Peg!" I hollered. But she had been hearing me say that to her ever since she was a pup. She knew that I was fixing to take it away, which meant to Peg, "I better down this thing pretty quick or I am going to bed without dessert." True to character, she started wolfing it down even faster.

I tackled her like a linebacker plugging a hole in a football game, and tried to wrestle the flare out of her mouth—but that made her even more determined. By the end of our scrum, all I got out of her mouth was about the last 2 inches of the 16-inch flare. The rest was in the process of being converted to calories, or whatever, in Peg's digestive tract.

Well, I don't know what's in a highway flare, but I am pretty sure that it isn't nutritious. I ran inside my host family's house, grabbed a phone book, and remembering that training I had when I was kid, started looking for the poison control emergency number. I found that number, and pretty soon had a lady on the line. She said, "Your dog ate a WHAT?"

"Really, I am not kidding, my dog ate a highway flare, and I need help," I replied.

"Well," she informed me, "I can't help you. What you need is the pet poison control hot line." She gave me the number that I anxiously wrote down and got it dialed. Another lady with a thick Brooklyn accent answered at the Pet Poison Control number. I guessed that she must have been on the East Coast, because it was late at night where I was at in Wyoming, and this woman sounded very tired—as though I had interrupted a pretty good dream.

However, she perked up after I related my story and exclaimed, "Your DOG ate a WHAT?" Déjà vu once more. Well, I had to tell her again that Peg had eaten a highway flare, and to reiterate my mounting concern I added, "Ma'am, I think this is fairly serious!"

I could hear her in the background thumbing through the pages of some reference manual while she asked me how much the dog weighed, the diameter of the flare, and any other pertinent information I could give her. Finally, there was this long pause, and she announced with authority, "You need to get this dog to the vet right away. This is bad stuff. This dog needs 32 ounces of slurried, activated charcoal." Slurried, activated charcoal, huh? I had never heard of such a thing, but the words stuck in my mind.

I thanked her and started dialing veterinarians with a Jackson Hole, Wyoming, address. I was obviously unfamiliar with anybody in the area, so I just went alphabetically down the list and dialed several numbers, where I got recordings. Well, it was midnight after all. When I finally got a live voice to answer the phone, I said, "Doc, I need 32 ounces of slurried, activated charcoal for my dog. She's just eaten a highway flare, and the woman at the Pet Poison Control Hot Line said I need 32 ounces of slurried, activated charcoal."

There was a pause . . . and the vet said, "Your dog ate a WHAT?"

I explained once again, "Really, this is no joke. I am here for the Rocky Mountain Stage Stop Race, and my dog just ate a highway flare."

To his credit, he took me seriously and told me to bring the dog right over to his clinic. He gave me directions, and I bolted back outside to gather up Peg for the ride over to his office. Before long, she was in the front seat next to me having a great time, thinking I was taking her to the Dairy Queen for a Blizzard or something.

Within thirty minutes of the time that Peg ingested the highway flare, I was pulling into his clinic's parking lot. The office lights were just coming on and, at this point, Peg was still showing no ill effects from her midnight munch. No indigestion, no (ahem) heartburn, just flat-out enthusiasm for life. I lead her out of the truck, and she was excitedly wagging her tail, thrilled with the opportunity to travel one-on-one with the Boss. As we went inside the clinic, I found that the sleepy veterinarian was now fully awake and all business.

He went right to work and started preparing this magic elixir I was hoping would neutralize the oncoming effects of Peg's snack. In a couple of minutes, the vet had mixed up a big bowl of the nastiest-looking muck you have ever seen in your life: a dark, gooey paste that looked like something you would suck up off the bottom of a pond. Blech. It definitely got my attention—my full attention.

Then he produced this long, clear tube and started slathering it with some kind of lubricant. I took a short breath, as I knew that tube was destined for one end or the other of poor old Peg. "Uh, what are we going to do with that?" I asked, not really wanting to know.

"Well," he explained as he worked, "we've got to get this thing down her throat so I can get this stuff down into her stomach. And we've got to do it as quick as possible!"

"Hmmm . . . Have you ever done this before?" I queried him.

"Oh, yeah, all the time, this should be no problem" he said with a lot more confidence than I had. "All you need to do is hold onto Peg, and I'll just slide this tube down her throat."

Yeah, right. I tried to hold on to her, but once she realized what the vet wanted to do, Peg said, "No way, no thanks, but this isn't going to happen." She started fighting with all her might.

"Wow, this dog is really strong," said the Doc, like he had just discovered something. I was thinking, "Well, yeah, she is one of the finest canine athletes in the world, and she definitely does not want any part of that tube." Peg was putting up the fight of her life, and there was no way that slippery, lathered-up tube was going down her throat. Besides, that 32 ounces of slurried, activated charcoal hadn't improved its appearance much—it was still looking pretty nasty.

Then it came to me. "Doc, do you have a dog dish?"

He looked at me like I was a total idiot. "Buddy, this is NO time to be joking around. This dog needs this stuff fast." He had this serious expression that communicated now was not the time for any silly distractions.

"Well, I think if we put this in a dog dish—she just might eat it!" I was trying to get Doc to come around to my way of thinking.

"She's not going to eat this stuff." He wasn't convinced. "Look at it!"

I turned my head once again for a closer scrutiny of the vile, black muck. From any reasonable person's perspective, there was absolutely nothing on the planet that was going to make that stuff appetizing to any normal dog. It was obvious that the vet was skeptical. I looked back up at him.

"Doc, she did just eat a highway flare!"

I let the idea settle into the deepest part of his brain. I didn't think he could maneuver around my logic.

"I really think it's worth a try," I added.

My instincts and credibility were on trial. He sighed and put down his plastic tube. After rummaging around under a counter, he found a large, stainless steel dog dish, and I took the 32 ounces of slurried, activated charcoal and poured it in. I then grabbed a handful of dog food kibbles that he had stored in the back room, and artfully sprinkled them on top like I was fixing a gourmet treat just for Peg. If there's anything I've learned from watching *The Iron Chef*, it's that it's all in the presentation. I brought the offering around to Peg.

"Oh, look what I have for you, Peg," I said in my kindest, most appetite-inducing voice. She instantly forgave me for the tube incident. Her tail was wagging. She was shifting her focus to just one thing—earning another A+ (and some bonus points to boot) on that shortlist of mine. As I set the bowl in front of her—before it even hit the floor—she attacked it, nearly splashing the contents as her nose dove straight into the bowl. She gobbled up that bowl of slurry and dog food like a vacuum cleaner, never even taking the time to evaluate the contents for flavor. The doc stood dumbfounded in sheer amazement. In an instant, she was licking the bottom of that bowl, her big, brown eyes looking up at me like she was just getting started and wanted another helping. Now.

Surely you are interested in the outcome of this story. Amazingly, Peg had absolutely no ill effects from eating that highway flare. Her appetite, which had gotten her into trouble, also got her out of trouble.

However the next day, as we were racing through the Rockies of Wyoming, I'm pretty sure that I saw a little flame shoot out her butt!

JOE'S NOTES

As Jeff has reminded us, a normal dog that's barking at the mailman and running around the neighborhood consumes only 1,500 calories a day. Meanwhile, on day eight or nine of the Iditarod, Peg is consuming calories at the rate of 8,000 to 10,000 per day. That's magic and precisely why she is a great dog.

But to me, the real message should be of great interest to anyone who owns and enjoys animals. It was no accident that Jeff turned the world upside down, looked inside Peg's brain, and came up with a spontaneous solution to a difficult problem. His dog was poisoned, and he had to find a way to save her—fast and without hesitation.

That he decided to defy common sense and just feed her a bowl of slurried, activated charcoal is an example of how he thinks upside down and comes up riding the sled standing up. I have seen him do it all the time. It's a strategy, a race philosophy, and a personality trait, to hurdle obstacles and overcome knots—and how to win.

CHAPTER FIFTEEN
Make a Wish

I n late 1995, the Iditarod Trail Committee came up with a
creative fund-raising idea that's become an excellent source
of revenue for the organization and a thrilling way for fans
to interact with the mushers. It's called the IditaRider Auction.

From November to January you can bid online for a chance
to leave the Iditarod starting line and ride down main street
Anchorage in the sled basket of your chosen musher. This opportunity would be comparable with sitting in the passenger seat for
a few laps in the Indy 500 or riding a thoroughbred on a warm-up
lap before the Kentucky Derby. Over the years, all kinds of people,
old and young, and even some famous personalities like actress
Susan Lucci, comedienne Joan Rivers and socialite Mary Lou
Whitney, have ridden a few miles with their favorite musher.

I've enjoyed the company of many fine people over the years,
but one IditaRider in particular, I'll never forget: a nine-year-old
boy named C. J. Kolbe.

It all began when I took the IditaRider concept to my sponsor,
Cabela's, the huge outdoor hunting and fishing supply, sporting

goods, and mail-order giant. I was thinking, *What a great way for Cabela's to encourage some employee involvement.* I pictured someone from the corporate offices, through some kind of incentive contest, rewarded with an all-expense trip to Alaska and the opportunity to ride with me in my sled.

One of the Cabela brothers, Jim, called me when the proposal hit his desk. "Jeff, I really like your idea," he said, "but I want to make one modification. We're not going to use it for an employee incentive. I want to donate it to the Make-A-Wish Foundation and see if they have some young person that might share this dream." Personally, I had no idea how that concept would later affect my life, but I immediately liked Jim Cabela's vision.

Meanwhile, on the other side of the continent in Broadalbin, New York, young C. J. Kolbe had recently lost his leg in his ongoing battle with cancer. The boy from the little Adirondack town of five thousand people had qualified for the Make-A-Wish Foundation program. His wish: to go to Alaska and ride in a dogsled.

The Cabela's offer and the wish of the little boy in Broadalbin circulated through regional offices, and eventually the two offers came together. I began receiving emails and letters from Cabela's indicating they had found a young boy who wished to ride in my sled at the start of the Iditarod.

I learned he was bald as a billiard ball and had lost one leg to his vicious disease. However, at the moment, he was in remission and his health was relatively good. As can be imagined, I had a lot to do preparing for the Iditarod, and I really did not have any direct communication with the little boy and his family—other than informative letters telling me who they were and where they lived. This all happened within six weeks of the Iditarod start on Saturday, March 2, 1996.

Cabela's and the Make-A-Wish Foundation of Alaska did a wonderful job organizing the family's trip to Alaska and planning all of the logistics for the race-start festivities. A rendezvous with the Kolbe family had been scheduled in Anchorage on the Thursday morning before the race. And later that night, at the Iditarod banquet, the Kolbes would be guests at the Cabela's banquet table and enjoy the presentations. The highlight of the evening, when mushers draw a start number out of a fur *mukluk* (an Eskimo-style boot), is the highlight of the banquet formalities. The Iditarod banquet is one of Alaska's biggest social events with over a thousand mushers, fans, and political VIPs (often including the Governor of Alaska), all gathered to celebrate this great pioneer tradition. Friday, the following day, was a rest day reserved for mushers' last-minute preparations for the Saturday morning ceremonial start on 4th Avenue, downtown Anchorage.

That Thursday morning, I remember waiting in the lobby of the Millennium Hotel, the official Iditarod race headquarters in Anchorage, and wondering who the Kolbes were. At that moment, two little blond-haired boys came bolting by like a couple of runaway horses, and a third one was not far behind, with one leg and crutches chasing his brothers down the hall—having a blast.

As it turned out, my three daughters were almost identical in ages with the three Kolbe brothers. Our two families had breakfast together, and within minutes the kids were talking together as if they had been long-lost friends. A couple of them were under the table clowning around, and the commotion quickly escalated. Soon they were excused from the breakfast table to go outside and play in the warm March sunshine.

That night, the Kolbes joined our entourage of Cabela's representatives, and I asked C. J. if he wanted to go with me to the front of the crowd on the elevated stage and help me draw my start number. He was clearly not interested in the press, which had been relentlessly following him—he had had enough of photos and interviews—but he thought the idea of going on stage with me sounded pretty cool.

C. J. and I walked together to the stage, which was set up on the main court of the Sullivan Sports Arena, and we stood together in the lights before a thousand people. I introduced him, told the audience about our friendship, and explained that C. J. was going to be my trail partner on Saturday. It seemed that C. J. considered his involvement with me as entirely his idea. Ours was not a contrived friendship. He was comfortable and confident being my trail partner and had absolutely no interest in sharing his feelings with the media. Later I learned from his mother that C. J. felt personally responsible for drawing my number and assumed the pressure to draw a good starting position. He already understood my strategy and also realized that most of the low starting positions had already been drawn. He knew I wanted a number to the front—say the top thirty—so that I could avoid the time-consuming problems in the early part of the race passing teams. C. J. beamed when he pulled number nineteen.

The next day, Friday, was our preparation day before the start on Saturday. For years, our family also has attended a wine and cheese pre-Iditarod sendoff at the Aurora Fine Arts Gallery in downtown Anchorage. Donna is a well-known artist in Alaska, and the gallery shows her extensive collection of wildlife and Alaska prints. Diane and Jerry, the gallery owners, are longtime friends and big supporters of our family and our Iditarod efforts. Hundreds of people attend this event, complete with big banners, to cheer "Jeff" on to Nome. Of course, we were there to mix with all of our supporters. C. J., his two brothers, and his parents were also at the gallery—they certainly didn't want to miss a party or any of the other festivities asssociated with the race.

In the middle of this fairly confusing and chaotic gathering of friends and fans, C. J. came up to me on his crutches, took a medallion out of his pocket, offered it to me, and with a big smile on his face, said, "Jeff, I want you to have my good-luck piece." It was an 1827 U.S. penny that had been given to him for good luck in his fight with cancer. He looked right at me, with the steady voice of someone who had already done a lot of living and understood what he wanted to accomplish. He announced, very matter-of-factly, "I want you to win the race."

I was stunned. In the midst of the background noise of a hundred talking people, I found myself in a true dilemma. If I accepted his charm, he wouldn't have it for the good luck he so obviously needed. If I took it and did not win—well, he might lose faith in a symbol that was helping him sustain his life. However I knew in my heart I had to take his offer of goodwill. I looked down at him, a little boy with so much kindness, and admit that I was in turmoil as I considered his generosity and the coin resting in the palm of his hand reaching out to me.

In an instant it came to me, "C. J., I don't want your good-luck penny forever, but I would like to borrow it. It's not because I want it to win the race, but I want your good-luck charm to help my dogs and me to stay healthy and safe. When I get to Nome, I'll send it back to you."

C. J. thought that sounded perfect, and his mom, with tears in her eyes, said, "I think it's perfect, too. I didn't know if I really wanted him to give it away."

I told C. J. that I would see him on Saturday morning for the big sled ride and shifted my attention to shaking hands for the next half hour and answering requests from the media for a few pre-race comments. Still, in the back of my mind, a persistent thought was giving me no rest: *How the heck am I going to keep from losing this thing?*

It was a practical consideration because I am notorious for losing things on the Iditarod Trail. I've flipped over and rolled my sled, slipped into overflow, darned near drowned crossing rivers, floundered in deep snow, gone days without sleep, and I knew that something crazy was likely to happen this year again. Eleven hundred and fifty miles across the wilderness of Alaska—how can I come up with a plan that will reduce my chances of losing

On the Trail to Shaktoolik, 1997 watercolor.

The 1996 Iditarod reported polar bear sightings along the coast. Jeff left the checkpoint of Shaktoolik alone and full of confidence, but later began to question his decision as he had nightmarish images of an encounter.

C. J.'s good-luck charm to zero? For a moment, as I struggled for ideas, I even imagined surgically implanting the charm under my skin as a failsafe plan.

His generosity and thoughtfulness touched me. Donna and I drove back to our friend Russell's residence outside of Anchorage in Wasilla, where we had the dogs and our equipment. We talked about C. J., and I explained the whole story to Donna about C. J.'s good-luck 1827 U.S. penny. At one point I told her, "I feel like I have won this race already. That was one of the most rewarding feelings I've ever had." Suddenly, winning the race did not seem so important to me any more. Any pressure that I might have felt to win paled in comparison to the pressure I now felt to make this a successful race for C. J. Most of all I wanted to have a clean and positive event, one that would make C. J. and my family proud of me.

By the time we arrived at Russell's place, I had a plan for securing the lucky penny. I'm pretty good at plans. I was going to cut the end off the finger of a glove, put that penny in the pouch, sew it shut, attach it to a ¼-inch rope, and tie that baby around my neck with a knot that wouldn't let loose unless my head came with it. Wherever I went, that coin was going to be coming with me. I was *not* going to lose it.

C. J. came to the start of the race on 4th Avenue on Saturday morning. He hated the press and found them a total annoyance. He did, however, manage to accomplish his own set of priorities— despite their constant intervention—and that was a single preoccupation with the dogs and his goal of helping his personal friend, Jeff King, win the Iditarod. He abandoned his crutches and scooted around in the snow with one leg so that he could visit each dog and touch and pet them with both hands.

The city of Anchorage hauls in truckload after truckload of snow the night before the race and literally lays down a man-made snow trail through the streets of Anchorage. Alaskan characters come out of the woodwork to join in the ceremonial Iditarod race start celebration. The Idita-Fairies are there in full fairy regalia, complete with oversized Bunny boots. Fur hats abound on the streets of Anchorage; one in particular that appears annually looks like a lynx that crawled up on the fellow's head and died there. Streetside vendors, can-can girls, the Idita-Chicks dressed in full-sized chicken costumes, and free coffee and hot chocolate available in the local shops all add to the electric energy on 4th Avenue. Spectators hang from upper-story windows, balconies, and the parking garages to get the best views of the departing teams.

For miles, the streets are lined with cheering crowds, some in lawn chairs, some organized into big outdoor barbecues, and they are all yelling encouragement, "Good luck, Jeff!" "Have a great race, Jeff!!" "Win it again!!!" and so on until you feel like you've waved at everyone in the state of Alaska. Along the trail we are offered home-baked muffins and hot dogs grilled "to go"—if you can get your team to stop there long enough. I am sure C. J. felt all that excitement and probably heard his name a few times, too.

While the other IditaRiders only rode about six miles, I took C. J. in the sled with me for the entire twenty-two miles to the Eagle River checkpoint. He was so emotionally involved with my Iditarod effort, I know it meant a lot to him. We had a great time together. A photo of C. J. and me, with his entire family beaming and waving in the background, is one of my cherished Iditarod memories.

I admit that there were moments in the next several days on the Iditarod Trail when I didn't think of him—but they were just moments. Mostly I thought about appreciating every day, my family, and our good health, and how C. J. had reminded me of those blessings. I was focused on making sound decisions along the trail that would get us to Nome healthy and safe.

As the race progressed over the next several days, an interesting realization began to appear. I was dominating the race and starting to leave the competition behind me. There was a real possibility that I was in a position to actually pull off a win. I kept checking the little pouch around my neck and rubbed the penny—*Yep, it's still there.*

As the teams approached the coast, reports filtered back of polar-bear sightings along the trail. Though it is rare to have these intimidating animals as far south as Unalakleet, the locals confirmed that it was not unheard of. It was the middle of the night in Shaktoolik when I was making my move to sneak out of the checkpoint, the first team on the trail heading across the sea ice to Koyuk. I heard the race checker calling to me and saw him waving a piece of paper in his hand. It was a recent fax from the Trail Committee warning mushers to travel together for safety along the coast due to the polar-bear sightings in the area. I made a hasty assessment in my mind. I knew that I was headed northeast, in the opposite direction of the sightings, and I was literally making my move to secure my place in front. I left the checkpoint alone with confidence in my decision.

It wasn't long, however, when in the darkness, every snowy mound began to resemble a crouched polar bear. I had left Shaktoolik worried a bit about staying awake for the 65-mile run to Koyuk, but with my imagination seasoned by worry, my senses were acute and my awareness was on high alert as my team and I traveled the coastal trail. "Dozing off" was far from even a remote possibility. I couldn't help but conjure images of an encounter with one of these huge, fearless arctic bruins.

Meanwhile C. J. flew out of Anchorage for another scheduled cancer treatment on the East Coast. While the race was on, and we were winding away across Alaska, C. J. was back in Broadalbin, New York. He said he would be checking on me, and I knew he would.

As it turned out, nine days, five hours, forty-three minutes, and thirteen seconds later, I won the Iditarod for the second time in my career. At the finish, someone who had been keeping in touch with C. J. and the Kolbe family told me that C. J. had not slept the day preceding the finish of the race. He had a telephone, TV, and computer beside his bed and was dialed in to the Iditarod.

Although he could not meet me in Nome, he did write a letter, which I received at the finish line. I read it out loud and it was broadcast over loudspeakers to the fans.

Hi, Jeff,

It's CJ. I knew you could win. I'm very proud of you. I thought of you the whole time. Do you know what the other mushers said? They said they can't catch you. Let me know what dogs finished the race. I hope to talk to you soon.

I love you, Jeff.

CJ

I wasn't prepared for the emotion I felt as I struggled to finish reading his letter. It was an incredibly powerful moment for me. I was able to call C. J. very soon afterward, and he picked up the phone after only one ring. I knew he was sitting there waiting for the call.

I sent the penny back to C. J. from Nome. That summer, the Kolbes came back to Alaska to celebrate C. J.'s birthday, and together we went on a fishing trip down in Homer, Alaska. But C. J.'s cancer was back, and he was very sick. Although it was difficult, we did manage to have a good time. Our families have remained good friends over the years.

C. J. cherished his penny in the leather glove tip and shoelace necklace. Over time, the memento collected dirt and started to get pretty ragged. Months later, I visited C. J. in Broadalbin, and at his mother's suggestion, cut open the glove tip. The penny was sent to a jeweler and mounted with a chain.

Almost a year after I met C. J., just a month before the 1997 Iditarod, he passed away. My sponsor, Cabela's, makes a personalized denim shirt for me with my name and "Iditarod" embroidered on the front. They also made one for C. J. that said, "C. J. Kolbe, IditaRider, Iditarod 1996." It was his request that he wear that shirt when he was buried, along with a stuffed husky he had received on his Alaska trip.

It is an incredible story and a very emotional experience for me. The following year I returned to his school in New York and gave the kids a presentation about the Iditarod, including C. J.'s experiences with me. It was a lot of fun, and I was fortunate to meet his friends.

The next year, I had another Make-A-Wish child share my sled with me and have had one for the last ten years—an un-expected, but very moving experience for my family and me. Certainly the Make-A-Wish Foundation, in partnership with Cabela's, has impacted families and children in ways we could have never imagined.

One thing, to set the record straight about C. J.: He was much more to me than a little boy with a heart-breaking medi-cal problem. C. J.'s mother shared a story with me after that magical Iditarod of 1996.

"I can remember my boys were talking with some friends in the car following the Iditarod," she said. "I was bringing a group of them home after one of Kyle's [C. J.'s brother] basket-ball games. All the boys were saying which major college they wanted to attend, and C. J. pipes in, 'Hell, I'm going to Alaska the day I graduate!'"

To this day, C. J.'s mother sends me the penny about a week before the start of the race. I have worn it every year and expect to keep the tradition as long as I run the Iditarod.

C. J. Kolbe was a friend, a remarkable chance encounter on the trail of life, an inspiration, and a very tough human being.

JOE'S NOTES

Through Cabela's and the Make-A-Wish Foundation, Jeff has added an emotional and inspirational element to the Iditarod that truly defines adventure. For updated reports on Jeff's trail partners and their Alaskan adventures, the reader can go to Cabela's at www.cabelasiditarod.com and www.iditarod.com. These are the children who have joined Jeff at the start line through the years:

1996   C. J. Kolbe, Broadalbin, New York

1997   Bobby Sipes, Everett, Pennsylvania

1998   Jacqueline Youngson, Texas

1999   Luke Holt, Anchorage, Alaska

2000   Rachel Fabrizi, Erie, Pennsylvania

2001   Reese Cherry, Alpharetta, Georgia

2002   Quinn Alsogoff, Kanehoe, Hawaii

2003   Angelo Grellis, San Mateo, California

2004   Heather Greenwood, Wasilla, Alaska

2005   Rachael Baker, Hanson, Missouri

2006   Keith (K. J.) Peck, Butte, Montana

2007   Tim Rau, Frazier, Colorado

CHAPTER SIXTEEN
A Promise Made

As much as I love the IditaRider program and my yearly commitment with Cabela's and the Make-A-Wish Foundation, I found myself in a sticky-wicket one year. My youngest daughter, Ellen, who is definitely one of "Daddy's little girls," found herself watching other people's kids ride in Dad's sled down 4th Avenue and was quietly observant. After a couple of years of this, Ellen climbed into bed with me the night before the 1998 race start and asked, "Daddy, why do you always take somebody else's kid in the sled, and not me?" She let the silence just kind of hang in the air.

You tell me: *How do you answer a question like that?* I had a lengthy moment of silence myself, trying to think of all the reasons that would make sense to a little girl, and finally abandoned all the complicated explanations.

"Ellen," I said, "these kids only ride with me at the start of the race. Why don't you meet me in Nome, and I'll let you ride across the finish line with me? How do you like that?" I had done my fatherly duty. She puffed up like it was a done deal.

Again, it's time for an admission. I am known to be an extremely focused individual. No question about it. If you want to stay to the front and be competitive, you have to stay unbelievably focused—and that's what I try to do. It was unusual that I thought of C. J. Kolbe so often on the trail in 1996. The emotional experience was just so powerful, I could not possibly ignore it. However, my little conversational interlude with Ellen was gradually pushed to the back burner of my brain by day two of the 1998 race. I admit it—it kind of slipped my mind.

Somewhere near the halfway point in the race, often in McGrath or Takotna, I usually take twenty minutes and try to give my family a call back at the Homestead—if I can find a phone and make a connection. It is the only time I break concentration during the race to check on the home front. I got Donna on the phone, and the talk quickly centered on my conversation with my youngest daughter.

"Jeff, what exactly did you tell Ellen?" asked my wife.

"What do you mean?" I had a lot to think about.

"You said she could ride with you at the end of the race?"

"Oh, wow. I did say that. She remembered?" I had created a situation. It is not a customary practice for people to ride in the sled at the end of the Iditarod.

"Does she *remember*? That's all she's talked about ever since you left!" Donna had one parting thought, "Well, I guarantee that she is not going to forget. Let's both do some checking on this, and why don't you try to get a message to me if you figure something out." The pressure was on.

Well, it did go through my mind—a couple of times—but I was intensely focused on my task. So, it might have slipped my mind once again—one of those things I could figure out later. The race was shaping up well for me and the team was running in the top three. I began to feel that we could have a shot at a third Iditarod victory and everything—except getting down the trail in the most efficient and competitive way—was shoved to the back of my mind.

As the race wore on, a brutal coastal storm was barreling out to the Bering Sea through the infamous Solomon Blowhole. This particular spot has a deep and tragic history that has been documented for more than a century. Countless travelers have struggled from marker to marker, reflector to reflector, as they made their way down the beach on their way to Port Safety just 20 miles from Nome. Approaching the Blowhole in daylight, we often see a curtain of windswept snow as it rushes off the mainland toward Siberia. Winds in excess of 50 mph are common. Rocks, driftwood, and gravel serve as the surface of the trail. Snow just can't hold on.

My lead dogs, Red and Jenna, charged into the curtain of howling, wind-driven snow. Both race veterans knew what was being asked of them, and they leaned into the wind as they guided the team in search of markers. Every several minutes I stopped the team and staggered from dog to dog, scratching away at the snow and ice that had accumulated in their fur and around their eyes. Their apparent gratitude encouraged me, and I did this often.

There's so much to think about in a coastal storm besides trying to win a dog race. It's dangerous, and you have to consider the welfare of the dogs constantly, as well as your own safety, not to mention losing the trail and blowing your chances to win the race. To do well, you can rely only on your good judgment and hope that the years of preparation are enough to overcome this obstacle. The last twelve hours en route to the finish line was an adventure of its own and one I will always remember.

But as quickly as the winds of the Blowhole began, they died again—exponentially. Relief flooded the team. As we approached the final miles to Port Safety, I realized that its name and location were not by accident.

We neared Nome in late morning and it became apparent that we were going to finish first in Nome at midday—we were

Cold Hands Warm Heart,
1994 watercolor.

A Yukon Quest print. An intimate moment along the trail that shows the interdependency of the dogs and musher.

going to win our third Iditarod! I swelled with pride as the team charged up the last incline over Cape Nome. It would be a decisive victory. When you come into Nome in midday as the winner, the word gets out. Every soul from up and down the coast of western Alaska is going to try and be there to welcome you. They come by airplane, snowmachine—and maybe even dog team—and find their way to the Front Street finish of the Iditarod. That might not seem like a lot of people, but when they are all side-by-side lined up on Front Street Nome, it is a rowdy crowd that will rival the end of any parade in New Orleans.

And by golly, the Idita-Fairies and Idita-Chicks are on the scene as well. It is like Mardi Gras in Nome. The whole community "puts on the dog," so to speak, with contests of all kinds: the wet T-shirt contest for the guys' entertainment, and the wet-buns contest for the ladies. Arm-wrestling, snowshoe races, the businessmen's dogsled race and even a golf tournament on the sea ice—complete with knickers, tams, and brightly colored balls so that you can find them on the ice. Nome has more taverns per capita that any other town in the U.S., and they are all brimming full, night and day, for the fun-filled week of the Iditarod finish.

The excitement on Front Street built while the crowds waited for news of a report on the progress of my team. It was like waiting for word from Apollo 13 as it was crossing through its silent re-entry phase. Fans were on the edge of their barstools, anticipating the news. Reports finally came from the spotters stationed at Farley's Camp, only 5 miles from the finish line, and as our team passed the historic Swanberg's Gold Dredge, the warning siren blared and the town buzzed.

About 2 miles out of town, the camera guys from the Alaska Superstation TV in Anchorage stopped me and asked if they could wire me up with a remote microphone so that the broadcasters could talk to me while making my "victory" approach to the finish line. They knew that I had an unassailable lead, and

I likely would have a bit of extra time to take care of the media. It is a nice formality and allows the winner to talk to the news-starved people of Alaska, who were watching the finish on a live, statewide broadcast.

The trail usually enters the confines of Nome on a locally used trail on the Bering Sea beach, then suddenly comes up a slip to Front Street. Here, the town police car, its lights flash-ing, greets the arriving teams and escorts them down the street, through crowds of people screaming and yelling congratulations, all the way to the finish chute. The veteran dogs know all about the finish and understand to follow the cop car.

This was my third Iditarod victory, so I also understood the ritual of coming into Nome in the lead position. It's hard to describe the combination of both relief and excitement that I felt that year. The storm and the effort that had taken so much of my concentration was now behind me, and I could literally *see* the burled arch that signifies the finish line.

About four blocks from the finish, however, our escort car sud-denly stopped. *Wait a minute,* I was thinking, *that's not in the script.* As I watched this development, the cop leaned out of the car, waved his arm, and shouted ahead, "OUT OF THE WAY!" *I've got to finish and he has a job to do.* "OUT OF THE WAY!" he repeated.

I could barely make out the small silhouette in a blue-and-yellow snowsuit, firmly planted in the street in front of the police car, facing the policeman with unfaltering determination. That very moment I heard a little voice, clear as a bell, announce, "But that's my Dad!"

To Ellen, her father's promise obviously overruled anything uttered by one of Nome's finest. The policeman looked back at me as if to say, "Well, you tell me what to do."

Ellen had not forgotten. I hollered, "Send her back to me!" She ran back and stopped in her tracks right beside the sled. Then all of the Iditarod fans in Nome and across the world had to wait while my seven-year-old daughter dug around in her pocket with her big mittens, fishing for something obviously very important.

"Dad, I have something for you!" she said. A cold Pepsi finally emerged from her pocket, and she held it up to me as if it were the big prize. I took it from her little hands and popped the top as she jumped on the sled runners. She rode to the finish in first place as I ran alongside the sled. Naturally I was proud as a peacock of my third win, but also of my daughter, who had stood her ground in the face of an undeniably intimidating mob of cheering fans, as well as a uniformed officer and squad car. A powerful line from my favorite Robert Service poem rang in my ears: "*A promise made is a debt unpaid . . .* "

Side by side, we traveled underneath the burled arch.

Joe's Notes

The last 77 miles of trail from the White Mountain checkpoint to the Nome finish line is in many ways the most difficult on the Iditarod trail. The wind is the cause. The most notorious and infamous blowholes are midway at the top of Topkok Hill and a wind tunnel that comes out of the mountains near Solomon. Topkok is barren tundra with the occasional patch of brush.

The people of Nome have placed spruce-pole tripods and even anchored metal-pole tripods as trail markers as a precaution for travelers. The Iditarod trailbreakers also put lathe into the wind-packed snow to mark the trail. Even with these precautions, however, ground storms often obscure the trail so as to make progress impossible. And worse, the storms often cheat, and simply upend the markers and tripods, and obliterate long sections of trail.

Finish Lines

Snow swirled like a frozen cyclone around me. Wicked, wind-blown snow assaulted my checks and nose like a thousand piercing knives. My mustache was a glacier of heavy frost and ice. My exhausted eyes squinted into the dark. The deep blackness of the Alaskan winter night squelched the meager light from my faltering headlamp. For years I had heard the coastal Natives call the wind "The Eskimo's Friend," but my roots went back to the golden hills of California.

I screamed into the freezing blackness: "Salem! Whoa, Salem!" My voice cracked with fatigue. *This can't be happening,* I thought. "Salem!!" The sound of my voice was sucked away by the drumbeats of the wind. Just seconds ago I had helplessly watched my dog team disappear into the invisible cloak of the arctic storm that was hammering the coast of Alaska. I stood breathlessly in disbelief. Fur from my ruff whipped my face as I stared down the drifted trail, seeing nothing.

I was in the lead of the 2006 Iditarod, just 300 miles from the finish line in Nome, and the unimaginable had just happened. As if I were in a suspenseful cliffhanger scene in an adventure film, I wondered, *How did I ever end up here?*

I staggered down the drifted trail as the tracks of my team were swiftly vanishing in the onslaught of the winds. I fought each heavy step as it was swallowed in the deep snow. My exhausted legs felt like lead weights as exertion and panicked adrenaline engulfed me. I screamed again against the winds to my lead dog, "Whoa, Salem, whoa!" The futility of my situation had become too real. I was asking for the impossible.

My dog team was most likely charging ahead in search of the meager protection of the spruce forest further down the trail. I had let my team down. My job was to hang onto the sled and to pilot them to safety. They needed me, and I desperately needed them.

Then, like a mirage emerging through the sweeping blizzard of snow, I saw the faint outline of something in the trail. I could barely make out the contour of what appeared to be the back of my sled. Unbelieving, I struggled forward, screaming again, "Salem, wait for me!"

I dug deep within for the energy to make the last lunging steps toward the security of my sled and team. My gloved hands finally clutched the hard wood of the sled handlebow. My heart raced with an overwhelming sense of relief and disbelief. *They had waited for me.* I slowly worked my way up through the team, petting and hugging each dog as I made my way to Salem. He stood tall and alert, watching my approach. I bent down and hugged him to me. His evident devotion went beyond words. I looked into his eyes, and his confidence and strength infused me with the power I needed to transform my fear back into the calm determination it would take to guide us to our fourth Iditarod victory.

It had been thirty-one years since I had first ridden a sled pulled by dogs. It was a snowy day in a Minneapolis city park, behind my older cousin's team of Siberian huskies. I remember the thrill like it was yesterday. The excited gallop of the powerful dogs. Snow sparkling on their silvery coats. Crouched and white-knuckled, I hung on with the excitement of a roller-coaster at the county fair.

Many miles of trail have swooshed under my runners since then. The team's charge down the street in Nome for our 2006 victory was a personal highlight for me. First to cross the finish line was Salem, followed by the quiet performers who make things happen: Houston, Texas, Tahoe, Bronte, and Dickens. Aspen, Angus, Berkeley, U Conn, and Bernard. Awesome as individuals; near mythological as a team. The satisfaction of being a part of this effort causes me to pause with reflection daily. Moments to be proud of oneself; moments to recognize those whose valuable support and effort, selflessly contributed, served like tracks for a speeding locomotive.

Sharing our life with tens of thousands of you who have visited our home at our Husky Homestead here in Denali Park has left us in awe as our lives cross paths with yours. I sincerely hope you have enjoyed your visit with us as much as I have enjoyed sharing our adventures with you.

Now with a family to be proud of, a wife I am in love with, and many good friends to share it all with, I go forward with anxious anticipation of the next race, whatever and wherever it will be.

Photo Album

I took a liking to dogs as early as 1958.

The King family piles on the couch for a group photo. From left: me, my father (John), Johnny, mother (Joan), and Joannie.

I was always bringing things home in my pockets. This was taken in about 1965, when I was in the fourth grade. I got to keep the snake for the weekend, then my parents made me put it back on the hill.

I was a sixth-grader when I trapped the fox that woke up in my pack. I used to wear a newspaper carrier's vest to haul all my gear. That's Sam, my trail partner.

That's me on the left with my brother Johnny. We helped build our log house in the summer of 1969.

Here I am in 1973, playing high school football. I'm pretty sure I threw a touchdown right there.

In the late 1970s, I achieved my dream of living in an Alaskan log cabin, running dogs, and trapping. Here I am with a wolverine and a lynx from my trapline caught on the same day.

Dennis Kogl, a friend who was a freight hauler, loaned me a team for this run, one of my first dogsled rides.

I built this cabin on the Homestead property in 1979 and lived there until about 1982, when I started work on our main house. It's still standing.

I had just finished a Knik Bay area race in about 1980, when photographer Jim Brown took this picture.
Jim Brown photo

My first sled, which I made from birch saplings and downhill skis.

In the late 1970s, one of my first jobs in the Park was working as a freight hauler for mountain climbers on Muldrow Glacier. That's Mount McKinley in the background.

ROLLIE OSTERIMICK PHOTO

Another photo taken in the late 1970s, from the days when I had a freighting business for Mount McKinley climbers. ROLLIE OSTERMICK PHOTO

My first Iditarod, the 1981 race, started at Settler's Bay instead of downtown Anchorage.

I didn't see her, but Donna stepped out of the crowd to get this picture as I left the 1981 Iditarod starting line.

In this photo from the early 1980s, I paused with Hickory during one of our regular training runs.

Donna and I were married on October 8, 1983, in Sandy Hook, Connecticut.

Me and our firstborn, daughter Cali, in Whitehorse before the 1985 Yukon Quest start.

The infamous Bull's Eye–Angel Creek run, moments before my team spotted the nice, long "runway" and shot down an icy road.

Hickory leading the way in the 1987 Yukon Quest. Notice how he's way out left on a long lead, and I'm deliberately tipping the sled in that direction, as both of us are working to direct the team into the wind. CHARLES MASON PHOTO

As Hickory aged, I could trust him to take the girls out for a ride. That's Cali on the runners; Tessa's in the sled.

My girls were standing on a sled (almost) as soon as they could walk.

The 1989 Yukon Quest finish, the year we all got thoroughly soaked in the Yukon River on the way to a championship.

Camping at the now-famous vehicle, known locally as "The Bus," which was abandoned on the Stampede Trail outside Denali Park many years ago. This was the site where Chris McCandless lost his life, his final days retold in Jon Krakauer's Into the Wild.

Daughter number three, Ellen, came along in 1992. Here, my girls and I set out for a little ATV adventure.

Our girls enjoying a game of, what else, dog mushing.

In more than twenty years together, Donna and I have made great partners.
JEFF SCHULTZ/ALASKASTOCK.COM PHOTO

*C. J. Kolbe was my 1996 IditaRider, a boy who made a
lasting impression in my life.*

*Red and Jenna led the team in the 1996 Iditarod. Here we're negotiating the treacherous
winds of the Solomon Blowhole.* Joy Berger photo

With C. J. in the sled, we greet the Kolbe family as we pass them in the Iditarod's 1996 ceremonial start. JEFF SCHULTZ/ALASKASTOCK.COM PHOTO

As media from around the world recorded our 1998 victory, my youngest daughter Ellen was there to greet her dad. She rode the runners while I jogged down Front Street in Nome.
Jeff Schultz/AlaskaStock.com photo

I was thrilled to be involved in shooting a commercial after my 1993 win. I gained great insight into the behind-the-scenes action.

Jake was my leader for the 1996 Kuskokwim 300 championship team. In all, I've crossed the Kusko 300 finish line first seven times.

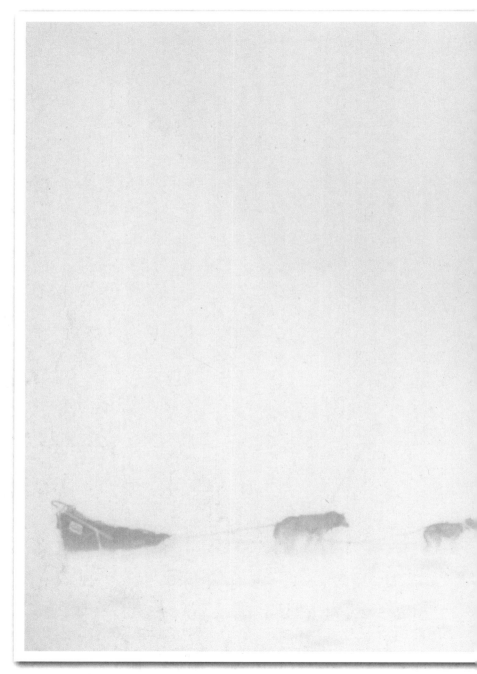

Coming out of the Solomon Blowhole in 1998, I had to move to the front to help my leaders.

Ellen was running her own trapline by 2000.

Tessa signing in at a checkpoint on the Junior Iditarod as she watches the competition leaving. Naturally, she'd follow ol' Dad's footprints, since she was born on Father's Day.

My girls posed for this picture in 2002, when Cali won the Junior Iditarod. From left, Tessa, Cali, and Ellen. Cali's leaders were Kansas and Potter (named the year the Harry Potter book was coming out).

This photo from 2003 shows one of my designs, the Caboose sled, in which I could bring along a crate. This way so I could alternately rest my leaders while we kept moving.

JEFF SCHULTZ/ALASKASTOCK.COM PHOTO

During the 2005 Iditarod start, I accepted a trailside snack of a hot dog as we cruised through Anchorage. My IditaRider was Rachael Baker, and that's Donna riding behind us in a trailing sled. A little extra weight helps slow us down—a little.

Jeff Schultz/AlaskaStock.com photo

On a training run around the Park in my Caboose sled; we're on our way to camp overnight at "The Bus." VIRGIL TROUT PHOTO

I may look like I'm sitting still, but notice the snow kicking up from the sled runners. We're moving through the village of Noorvik at about 10 mph, and on our way to winning the Kobuk 440 in 2005. That was my new Taildragger sled design. MARK NORDMAN PHOTO

In 2001, a group of Iditarod champions gathered for a photo under the famous Burled Arch, the finish line in Nome. From left: Doug Swingley (1995, 1999, 2000, 2001); Dick Mackey (1978); Jeff King (1992, 1996, 1998, 2006); Martin Buser (1992, 1994, 1997, 2002); Rick Swenson (1977, 1979, 1981, 1982, 1991); and Rick Mackey (1983). So far, Swenson is the only five-time champion. Jeff Schultz/AlaskaStock.com photo

Our motel on wheels is pretty comfortable for dogs and driver. Here, the dogs are picketed around the truck on short chains that allow them to snack and stretch their muscles without getting tangled.

The second King to run the Iditarod was my daughter Cali at age 18. Here's the two of us passing each other head on in the 2003 race. That year, low snowfall in Southcentral Alaska created a problem for Iditarod race organizers. They had to alter the course, starting in Fairbanks, racing down the Yukon and making a return trip on part of the trail.
Jeff Schultz/AlaskaStock.com photo

Visitors who come to the Husky Homestead get a lesson in the unique qualities of the Alaskan husky, and what it means to train year-round. We demonstrate training runs using a four-wheeler for our guests. It's something we do four times a day, 125 days in a row each summer.

After our 2006 win, I initiated a swimming program inspired by a line in Lance Armstrong's training book: "There's no such thing as an off-season."

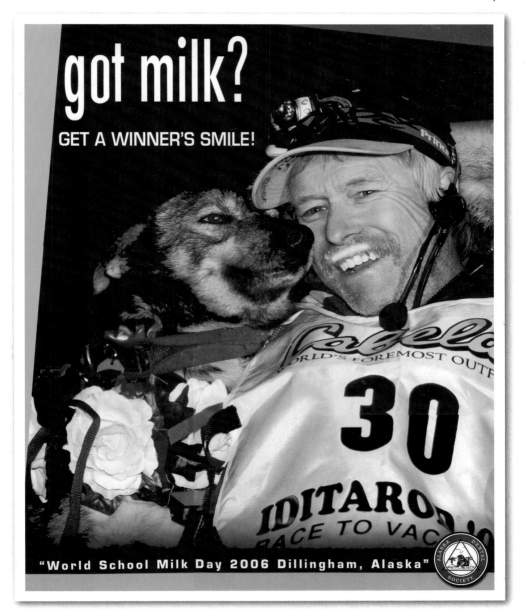

*Salem, my 2006 Golden Harness Award winner, posed with me at the finish line
that year of my fourth win. The image by Iditarod photographer Jeff Schultz was
used as a regional promotion in the "Got Milk?" campaign.*

The Iditarod starts on the first Saturday of every March, and once we set off from Anchorage to Eagle River, everybody's glad to be running.
Photo by Jeff Schultz/AlaskaStock.com

Gotta wear shades.

*This is Deets taking over and having fun at Goose Lake Kennel
in the summer of 2007.*

Here's Call, ready to rip out for a daily training run.

When we started the Husky Homestead Tours in 1992, we had 200 people that first year; these days we get more than 26,000 visitors each year.